Chronicles of a Motorcycle Gypsy: Dirt Bikes and Dinosaur Bones

By Tiffani Burkett

First Printing, 2021

I have tried to recreate events, locales and
conversations from my memories of them. In order to
maintain their anonymity in some instances I have changed
the names of individuals and places, I may have changed
some identifying characteristics and details such as
physical properties, occupations and places of residence.

ISBN: 978-0-578-94601-6

*

Book Design and Cover by Tiffani Burkett

Photographs by Tiffani Burkett and David "Hollywood"
Hayward

Other Books by Tiffani Burkett

- *Chronicles of a Motorcycle Gypsy: The 49 States Tour*
  ISBN: 978-0578212838

- *Chronicles of a Motorcycle Gypsy: South of the Border*
  ISBN: 978-0578578101

- *Chronicles of a Mermaid*
  ISBN: 978-0578803562

- *Taffy's Tales: Adventures in Costa Rica*
  ASIN: B07SFZDGXR

- *Zombies Don't Eat Catnip*
  ASIN: B098VZ3TK2

Prologue

Seven thirty in the morning and my phone was already ringing. Hollywood had left for work no more than twenty minutes ago. He'd probably just arrived, actually. He should have still been in the process of "Good Morning!" and "How was your Thanksgiving?" type small talk with whoever was in the office. I glanced around as I set aside my latest manuscript until I located the offending ringer. I tugged the phone from the charger and paced into the living room, trying to deduce what he was calling for. He didn't leave his laptop behind. He had his hard hat and vest. Odd.

I shrugged and answered the phone. "What's up, babe?"

"Can you come pick me up?" The question was ominous, but his voice was almost sing song as he said it.

"Of course. What happened?"

"They let me go. Just turned in the keys to the company pickup."

"I'll be right there."

Ten minutes later, I arrived at Hollywood's office, and he greeted me with a smile as he hopped into the passenger seat of our old Chevy truck.

He gave me a quick peck on the lips and shrugged. "I was starting to hate that job anyways."

I nodded. "Yeah, I could tell. No big loss."

I rubbed his shoulder then I pulled out of the parking lot to head back to our little apartment in Boise, Idaho. The eighty hour weeks he'd been working had given me plenty of time to focus on my own work, but he had just about never come home happy. Though that's what it takes to save up enough money to take off months and months to travel sometimes. While in the past, I had always been the one hustling to save up money while working various soul sucking software development jobs, this time around we had approached rebuilding our finances a little differently. Over the last year, he was grinding away at an Engineering job, and I was grinding away to establish a more serious writing career that could become a passive income that sustained us while we were actively on the road.

But after a year and a half, our account had recovered to a more than reasonable level, and my books and freelancing gigs were making us enough to cover basic living expenses.

I pulled into our driveway, put the truck in park, then I turned to Hollywood before I turned off the key. "I guess that means it's time to finish riding around the world."

"Yep."

Preparing to travel around the world tends to be more of a mad scramble than any of the methodical, well thought out planning you might imagine. It's a lot of "where do you want to go, anyways?" and "Can we get visas for that country?" and "Have you seen my base layers?" Or in Hollywood's case, it was more along the lines of "Oh yeah, I should probably actually get a motorcycle license."

We ended our lease in Boise on the last day of January and shoved everything we still had into a storage unit. Then we loaded up the pickup with our motorcycles, namely my 2015 Yamaha FZ-07 and his 2003 Yamaha FZ1, and we made our way over one high elevation, snow covered pass after the other to get from Boise to Denver.

6

It was an odd feeling as we drove away from that warm and comfortable apartment we'd been living in for a little over a year. It was relief, as we put a stressful life of hustling and extreme penny pinching behind us (not that we penny pinch much less on the road), but it was also an intense anticipation as we stared down what was supposed to be the start of a trip that would take an uncertain number of years through an uncertain part of the world. Did we have enough money? What would the roads be like in Africa? In Siberia? Would we survive these new challenges? Would the people be kind?

Were we ready?

Is anyone ever really ready for a ride around the world?

Probably not. But at least with our previous two year, 60,000 mile, multi-country trip under our belt, it felt wholly possible.

The day started about how you would expect a day in my life to start, with a semi-truck jack knifing right in front of us, as it buckled and slipped atop winter conditions. By the time we made it to Salt Lake City, stopping at In N Out for dinner like any red blooded Californian should, the I-80 was closed due to wind and snow.

The I-80 is always closed when I head this way. I'm not sure if that highway is ever open, actually. We rerouted through Vernal and Steamboat as a result. I was used to that route by now, so with the exception of having to sleep out the night in the sub-freezing temperatures after realizing it was far too dark to see the abundant herds of elk, we made it up and down Poudre Canyon with little to do.

Our flights to Morocco were already booked for the beginning of April—the earliest we could get our bikes on a plane for the "Fly Your Bike" program through Air

Canada. So we had two months to secure our Russian Visas and for Hollywood to secure a legal M1 Driver's License. He had ridden all the way from Alaska to Panama with little more than a permit, and I wasn't confident that Europe would offer the same leniency for missing credentials as Latin America.

It took about three weeks to get his license. Not because of the DMV or the slow mail service. But because the moment we arrived in Colorado, we ended up getting snowed on just about every day. Like clockwork, it would snow all night, melt off by the afternoon, then snow all night again. As such, the license exams were all closed down until they could get a sunny enough day to have a dry parking lot.

When he finally did get to go in for his exam at a local Harley dealership, much to my amusement, the instructor saw me standing at the counter and walked right past Hollywood.

"Can I get a signed copy of your book?" He asked without wasting any time on formalities.

"Only if you pass him today." I chuckled in response. Not that Hollywood needed any help. He'd been riding since he was a little kid. He was so effortlessly good on any motorcycle he threw his leg over that it was actually annoying.

I let him take the class on my FZ-07, which he passed with flying colors, then with goodbyes said and Hollywood the most legal he's probably ever been in his life, we were off to tie up the remaining loose ends. We went to California to apply for our Russian Visas, which cost a solid thousand dollars of our budget, and I got to say goodbye to some of my friends who I hadn't seen in nearly three years. I'd often wanted to move back to Southern California in the last three years, but I also often feared that

8

if I settled back in with these wonderful people I knew and loved, I wouldn't want to leave. Being in other places kept me focused on my goal. I would come home just as soon as I finished.

Confident and ready, we made our last stop in Phoenix, Arizona with my mother, where we would finish up any remaining preparation. Oil changes, new chains and sprockets, coolant and brake fluid flushes. All the normal, basic pre-trip maintenance. With two weeks to go, we verified all of our luggage. Double checked tickets and reservations. Bought new base layers and broke in new riding gear. We began loading up our saddle bags to head up to Vancouver, Canada and catch our flights to Africa.

And that's when everything went to shit.

Look how cute and ready these bikes are. Who's going to be the one who has to tell them they don't get to go on adventure? (Castle Hot Springs, Arizona)

Chapter 1

Two more weeks was all we needed. That's it! On a cosmic scale, that's less than the blink of an eye!

But two weeks had taken on a new meaning. Instead of being an exciting amount of time that would move entirely too fast, until I was begging for just one more day to get ready, it became the amount of time we had to lockdown in quarantine. It was the amount of time the Coronavirus was supposedly contagious, and the amount of time we needed to stay cowering inside our homes, so as not to risk exposure.

Just two weeks.

I held out hope. I had worked and lived through scares for SARS and H1N1 and all the other various strains of animal born respiratory illnesses, so what was one more? I had never seen the whole country shut down and start wearing masks before, but surely after those two weeks, the world would right itself again, and we could get on that plane. The economy couldn't possibly survive otherwise. So… Surely…

I refused to believe it was as serious as it was up until we got a phone call from Air Canada cancelling our shipment to Morocco, not simply for a few more months but for the rest of the year.

The rest of the year? What happened to two weeks?!

There had to be another way to still do this trip, I thought. I looked up boats, and crating my bike to ship out of the US. I looked at shipments out of Mexico instead of Canada. I looked up routes through Africa, in case Europe was closed for a little while.

But as one border after the other slammed in our faces, no amount of hope and denial and alternates plans came to matter. There was no "let's go here instead" or "let's ship this way." Nor was there a "let's get jobs again and beg for our apartment back." Every door closed, one after the other, until all there was left was my mom's couch, a pit of depression, and endless, mind numbing Netflix marathons.

I love escapism and fantastic stories as much as the next nerd, but living vicariously through other people was hardly how I wanted to live my life anymore. Not when we had spent so much time and effort to travel around the world ourselves.

Two fucking weeks!

That was all I needed so I could have instead... been stuck in quarantine in third world Morocco.

Well... I'm not sure if that would have been better or worse, actually.

Still, I love my mother more than anyone in the world, but moving back in with her wasn't really one of my after-thirty life goals.

I held out and fought and cried and screamed and hoped things would get better for as long as I could, but by the end of April, nearly two months into the start of the pandemic shut downs, a decision had to be made. If we couldn't get jobs in this world of sudden mass-unemployment, and if we couldn't travel in the equally depressing world of international border closures, what were we going to do so we didn't go completely and utterly mad?

We had a lot of our own country we could explore, but after touring 49 states over nearly an entire year, it was hard to get excited about just repeating the same trip.

Riding around our own country was just too easy now. We spoke the language, gas was never far away, camping was safe, food and water were generally safe—the ante had already been upped in Latin America, and to backtrack now just sounded like a waste of that hard earned savings. I needed a challenge.

And besides, in lieu of all the closed campgrounds and national parks, the most majestic and awe-inspiring portions of our country weren't accessible anyways. Even if I wasn't becoming a bit of a masochistic snob, this was hardly the best time to explore the USA either.

Our country was all we had though, so the only thing to do was to find a way to make it interesting again. After a lot of arguments and denial and coin flipping, the ultimate decision was to spend the summer riding dirt bikes around the US, as both a way to explore new places we couldn't (or I wouldn't) go on my sport bike, and to finally force me to become a half way competent dirt rider. My street skills had long been polished and refined, but my dirt skills had never really gotten off the ground.

Or rather, my dirt skills often threw me on the ground.

I had planned to work on those as we rode across Siberia, but I suppose this was a wiser place to do that, anyway.

We fortunately already owned a KLX125, making the priority shift that much more reasonable. We had bought this little kid's dirt bike in Montana, where we had studded the tires with sheet metal screws in order to pass the many, many, many, many winter months riding on frozen lakes. It was short enough that I could comfortably touch the ground, slow enough that it was completely unintimidating, and light enough that I could easily pick it up, even if I ended up in an "upside down in the sand, mud, and rocks" situation. A most perfect learner bike for an anxious, uncoordinated, and easily scared rider.

But as riding two-up on a three foot tall, eight horsepower bike wasn't that practical, we started shopping around for a second dirt bike for Hollywood. It took about a week before he stumbled upon a 2010 Kawasaki KLX 250. The selling price was higher than I would have expected for such an understated dual sport, but upon walking into the seller's garage, where he had a shiny new Yamaha FZ-07 in the corner, he was quick to let us haggle him down a thousand dollars in exchange for a signed copy of my book.

Who says life as a starving artist doesn't have perks?

With Hollywood suited with a new steed, we headed back to Boise to get our KLX125 out of storage for me to use.

Neither one of us had dirt bike gear though, so I found myself digging out an old ADV kit. I grabbed some gear that was incredibly functional but had never fit me as well as I wanted it to. It would be safe to use, but it was also something I wouldn't feel bad about ruining in a slow speed get off.

With two bikes, an old Chevy pickup, armored Gore-Tex, and new inspiration, we pointed our nose toward the beautiful but treacherous Rocky Mountains in Colorado.

Where better to start my dirt bike boot camp?

The KLX250 was an incredibly capable bike, but it was also big and heavy enough to give Hollywood a little bit of a handicap in the hard stuff, so he wouldn't completely leave me in the dust (Spoiler: He was still able to leave me in the dust) (Phoenix, Arizona)

Chapter 2

The drive back to Colorado was as long as it always is. Well, at least this time I wasn't doing it in a blizzard. A lot of caffeine got us all the way to Silverthorne, where we had a bed to sleep in with Hollywood's best friend, Dennis.

Dennis was a mechanic and fellow motorcycle racer, who I had, naturally, met at the racetrack. I hadn't realized how close he and Hollywood were before we took off on our first journey, but after he had been there to help us out throughout the entirety of our Alaska to Panama tour (and answer a surprising number of drunken, late-night phone calls), there was little question. When I had first met him, he was running a shop out of Westminster, just outside Denver. But life had taken him to Summit County, where he now lived with his girlfriend, Carolanne, surrounded by endless circuits of some of the most beautiful scenery and trails that Colorado had to offer.

I had only met Carolanne very briefly at this point, but her natural charisma and no nonsense attitude made her a fast friend. She wasn't a motorcyclist at all—her power sports passion rested more in the realm of snow mobiles—which incidentally made her the perfect companion to learn to ride dirt with. I had a bit of a one up on her in terms of using the hand controls, as over a decade on a street bike had made clutching with my hand and shifting with my foot second nature, but what she lacked in experience, she made up for with a can-do attitude. More of a can-do attitude than I had at times, honestly. The speed and terrain of sledding had given her a solid foundation for dirt riding, and like most people, her fear threshold was much higher than mine.

We were only in Colorado for about a day or two before we were taking the bikes to an OHV park. Not even enough time for my body to fully adapt to the bloating and headaches that often plagued me for the first week at high altitude.

Silverthorne was poised at 9000 feet, while we had come up from living at sea level over the course of a single day's drive, and the change in atmospheric pressure had taken its toll. It never affected Hollywood much, having spent most of his life at a mile high, but it was fairly inevitable for me, as someone who been born and raised about 20 miles from the ocean.

Unfortunately, Dennis wouldn't be coming with us for this first outing. My usual bad timing had us showing up the day before he left to go race with a club in Utah. But it was no worries, as Carolanne was more than game to go with us in his stead. If anything, it might have been easier for her first time riding her dirt bike to be without the eyes of her partner.

It could just be a *me* thing, but I'm always a lot more self-conscious about doing just about anything when someone is watching me. I don't mind making mistakes on my own, but the potential for failing in front of someone who I want to impress is the kind of burden that tends to make me mess up even more. Hollywood is used to me face planting into rocks on a regular basis at this point, but that doesn't mean I don't still have aspirations to make him believe I'm 1% cool when I ride. So in that way, going with just the three of us might have been the easier introduction to what was about to be a long and turbulent summer.

The weather that weekend couldn't have been nicer. We woke up on a sunny, low 70s day, with a breathtaking view of Quandry in the background, one of Colorado's many fourteeners. Herds of elk slept in distant plains outside our window, only separated from us by a willow lined creek meandering through the neighborhood.

Hollywood and I each took one side of the bed to straighten out the blanket, when Hollywood hollered. "Oh look, a moose!" He nodded toward the window.

"Where?!" I turned around quickly, hoping to catch one of these elusive—if not mythical—creatures, but all I could see was the overgrowth of bushes surrounding the creek.

"Just kidding. But it looks like there could be one out there," he said with a shrug.

My expression flattened, and I returned to shaking out the blanket, now with the mild aggression of disappointment.

No sooner had the comforter wafted down to the sheets below, did my peripheral vision catch the sight of a small bull moose sprinting past the window.

"Moose!" I pointed, dumbstruck, with my mouth agape.

"See, told you." Hollywood managed to laugh through his similar levels of shock. After going all the way from Alaska to Maine, camping in the mountains of every state in between, I had started to believe that Big Foot and Unicorns were more likely to be real than these alleged "Moose" that everyone kept talking about. So to see one on our first day of riding in Colorado was probably a good sign.

Buzzing from the morning, we loaded up my KLX125, Hollywood's KLX250, and Carolanne's Honda CRF150R with little urgency. We meandered with a pan full of eggs and bacon until half past ten, watching the moose chewing on the willows out the window, then off we went to the most beginner friendly trail system we could find.

The town of Kremmling wasn't far from Silverthorne. Well, calling it a town may have even been a bit generous. A small fraction of its real estate was comprised of small, humble homes and a couple mom and pop restaurants. And the bulk of the land was an OHV park. The climate was more desert-like than I had expected from this part of the world, especially after coming from the unapologetically green high alpine world of Breckenridge and Silverthorne, but desert is where I come from, so desert is fine with me. We unloaded the bikes, and I pulled on my worn out set of adventure gear.

This wasn't my first time ever on a set of knobbies or anything. Aside from the ice racing in Montana and the couple hours of bumbling around a dirt parking lot in Idaho, I had actually tried to learn to ride a dirt bike really early in my riding career. I had started riding sport bikes in the Spring of 2009, I started doing track days in Spring of 2010, then I bought my first dirt bike in November of that same year. I knew barely more than nothing about off road bikes at the time, so since I had started out riding on a Ninja 250, I determined that I needed at least a Honda CRF230F for the dirt. The CRF150F would have been a far better option, and likely one that would have had me continuing to ride dirt bikes beyond that first attempt, but I had little understanding of things like height and weight and horsepower needs in situations of low traction and mediocre balance.

It took me a few months to find the bike, and when I did, it was from a dad who was selling it for his twelve year old son who had decidedly outgrown it. I almost felt a little embarrassed to be a 22 year old woman taking on a vehicle deemed not good enough for a twelve year old, but obviously, based on my current bike choice (The KLX125), I have long since wised up on that ridiculous insecurity.

But 22 year old Tiff had an ego, however small it may have been, and it was just prevalent enough to make me feel awkward about buying a motorcycle hand me down.

But that "Maybe I'm too experienced for a bike this slow" notion was quickly dispelled when I threw the bike on a trailer and dragged it out to a large OHV park about 80 miles north of LA. Like most of Southern California, Gorman (Also known as Hungry Valley) was a desert climate. The terrain makeup was a combination of hard packed dirt, sand, and gravel, decorated with sage brush and maybe the occasional cactus or Joshua tree.

I put on a full suit of armor's worth of gear that cost more than the bike itself, then off I went.

Immediately I felt awkward. The ground seemed to move beneath me independent of the bike, and it was so tall, I could barely touch a toe down without scooting to one side. The brakes were squishy and I didn't know which one I was supposed to use, and that 18 horsepower engine felt like tremendously more power than I had any business using now that I was in the weeds. No part of this bike felt comfortable. It certainly wasn't like the bike I had gotten used to in the canyons or on the race track. I'd never wished so hard that I could have a mentor for this style of riding, but like so many things I've done in life, I was on my own and had to figure it out.

Maybe I just needed to try some trails and it would start to feel more comfortable, I reasoned. I started with the basic fire road that connects the trailheads and camping areas of Gorman, where traction was steady and predictable. Riding in a straight line over only the smallest imperfections or washboards started to fool me into thinking that dirt bikes were easy. I stood through the whoops, using my legs as suspension, then I turned down my first trail.

I made it a good mile, riding through lightly banked berms on an easy green circle beginner trail. I could do this. Dirt bikes weren't so bad.

Then after a few twists and turns, the trail opened up into a wash of loose sand.

As quickly as I had gained confidence, I lost it all as my bike wiggled and squiggled through a traction-less mess, before unceremoniously plopping me onto the ground. The one, and I maintain *only*, good thing about sand is that at least it doesn't usually hurt when you fall in it. My armored body hit those eroded little rocks like bouncing on a sandpaper covered pillow. No problem, I thought.

But it turns out, the CRF230F is kind of a big pig of a bike. At 250 pounds wet, in the soft surface of deep sand, me having all the strength of a scrawny nerd, and with bulky, stiff, brand new dirt bike boots restricting my every movement, I had a hell of a time getting that bike upright again. I'd huff and puff until I got it up to knee height, only to have the bike sink into the soft surface and slide away from me. Rinse and repeat, until by some sudden miracle of tears, tiny muscles, and unexplainable leverage, I got that awkward paperweight on its wheels again.

But being a pretty new rider still, it didn't take long before I killed the battery trying to start a bike with a flooded carburetor. The 2005 model had no kick starter for backup—not that I would have known how to kick the bike anyways (and the concept of bump starting wasn't even in my vocabulary yet)—so I walked my bike back to my car, defeated, stumbling in my heavy boots, and trying not to trip over the rocks and ruts and end up dropping the bike on its side again. I don't think I would have had the strength left in me to get it back up.

Needless to say, I joined a gym after that debacle. Life as a video game nerd was not serving me well in motorcycle land. But more significantly, I also decided that dirt bikes just weren't something you should be out there riding alone. Learning to ride street on my own had been easy enough, at least in the sense that if I dumped my bike in an awkward place, there was just about always a guaranteed audience around to witness my failures and help out, much to my relief (and dismay). Additionally, since the grip of tarmac was largely predictable and easy to manage, the instances of dropping said bike were much fewer and further in between.

But dirt felt like a team sport. If you hurt yourself in the middle of an expanse as large as the Mojave Desert, for example, you could easily be lost if no one else happened to take the same random route through the same patch of sand that day. It was easy to end up in places wild and unexplored, so without a single friend who rode off road to ask for companionship or advice, I put the bike back in my garage, and forgot about it for a few years. I was enjoying riding track and street enough that I didn't really feel like I was missing much. My time and money were already fully dedicated elsewhere.

Well, until four years later when a racer friend of mine asked me to go to Gorman with him. He had just gotten a new Kawasaki KLR 650, a massive tank of a bike, and he wanted to start getting used to it. He had planned to quit his job and ship the bike down to South America to ride back up from Tierra Del Fuego the following year, so for him it was a trial run. As I was the only one he knew with a dirt bike, it only made sense to ask me to come along. We loaded up and headed out together.

Back at Gorman, but now with far more years of road racing and canyon riding under my belt, I was much less anxious this time. Well, at first anyways. He led the way and I followed, as the blind led the blind through a bunch of desert trails that all looked largely the same. I was doing much better at keeping the bike upright this time, but when we approached our first hill climb, his natural confidence took him right to the top, and my overthinking and lack of momentum stalled the bike mid hill. I still couldn't really touch the ground very well on that bike, having incidentally not gotten any taller since the last time I rode it, so in a series of mistakes, I ended up in a bush, while my bike plopped upside down on the incline.

Fortunately I had someone to help me up, but my already delicate confidence was now shaken.

We continued the ride to another fire road, where my buddy took off at a speed much faster than I had any interest or mental capacity to go. A few forks in the road later, even his dust trail was long out of sight, and I had to start making my own guesses on which way he might have gone.

I took a turn that lead me into a dried river bed, where I wrestled my handlebars through whoops of loose chunks of gravel. The further I went, the more lost I was. I had certainly taken a wrong turn at some point, but I couldn't say where, and turning back in all this gravel wash to figure that out was scantly more appealing. I was both afraid of dropping the bike, and afraid of ending up somewhere I'd never find my way back from, but with no other options, I persevered. Though I was starting to think I may as well have just come here alone if this is how it was going to go.

It was on a prayer of whoever answers the prayers of atheists that got me back to the truck. He met me there shortly thereafter, and he waved for me to follow him again.

At this point, I probably should have given him a piece of my mind, but twenty-five year old Tiff had the backbone of a particularly floppy jellyfish, and instead, I apologized for being a burden, and tried yet again to ride some trails with him.

He was feeling confident now, so he didn't hesitate to turn off onto a trail marked as a one-way black diamond.

He took off and I followed him up a narrow road that wrapped along a mountainside. As we climbed higher and higher, I found my peripheral vision tugging at me to look at the cliff beside me. As we got higher still and the desert plants were no longer hiding the cliff exposure, I couldn't help myself.

Panic.

In a split second, my mind calculated every single thing that could go wrong, and in a slightly longer second, I crashed into a wall.

The bike was still upright, thanks to, well, the wall, but my mind wasn't repairable. The road wasn't even that skinny, easily being wide enough for an ATV, but my lack of confidence in my ability to control the bike even with that much room for error cannot be understated.

He circled back on foot to find where I had disappeared to again, and he agreed to let me lead this time. The first seemingly kind and rational companionship I had been offered all day.

But it didn't matter at that point. The series of upsets had my mind rattled and unfocused, and I crashed into every berm and bush and rock that I somehow found. By crash number eight, as he chucked my broken fender into the brush, we determined that it was time to call it a day.

Fortunately, the downhill portion of the trail was much easier, and I was able to calm my hyperventilating panic attack down enough to get myself back to the truck in one piece and with only moderate trauma.

My riding companion wasn't tired yet, though, so he opted to take my 230 and do some laps around the peewee MX track by the parking lot. I hung out and watched, while he got bolder and bolder on the little bitty jumps.

Lap five, he had gotten just a touch too bold. He rounded a bend, then took the next jump as fast as he could make that heavy bike go, not accounting for the lack of real estate for catching air on a full size motorcycle.

Needless to say, it didn't end well. He pitched my bike into one hay bale, and pitched himself into another. The day ended with bent handlebars and a freshly broken wrist.

One week before we were both set to fly to Colorado for a road race no less.

Since he had crashed on *my* bike, and he had only come out to Gorman "because of me," immediately he made it clear that his injury was all my fault, and I needed to take responsibility for it. Whatever that meant. Again—twenty-five year old Tiff: meek and always apologizing, so I agreed that I'd do whatever I could to make it up to him. He made no effort to hide his disdain as he backed the truck up to the loading ramp, where I stood in horror as I realized this also meant that I now had to load a CRF230 *and* a gigantic tractor of a KLR 650 into the back of the truck by myself.

Good thing I had started going to the gym all those years ago, eh?

I'll just say thank-fucking-god Gorman has big dirt platforms for easy loading. But trying to handle that hulking beast of a motorcycle through the wooden fencing to get up the ramp was still a feat and a half.

Not a great second impression of dirt bike life, and not a great riding companion. After that day, I was about done with this whole dirt thing (and incidentally, that friendship ended shortly thereafter, when the following race weekend in Colorado turned into one of the worst of my life).

I accepted after that ride that off road, indeed, wasn't for me. I hated it, and there were more than enough actually fun things I could do on a motorcycle, that I didn't see any reason to expend further time or resources on it. I was getting plenty of riding time at the race track, and riding motorcycles is way too dangerous a hobby if you're not even having fun.

The 230 went back to sitting in the back of my garage, collecting dust and sadness. A few more years later, I ultimately sold it, replacing it with a Kawasaki KX65 mini bike with supermoto tires, adult suspension, and full-sized handlebars that I could race on paved go-kart tracks instead.

Ironically, a decent number of my other road racing friends suddenly bought dirt bikes shortly after I sold that stupid thing, but I'm not one to hold grudges or anything.

Fuckers.

Anyways, back to the present, I now had the little KLX125, which I could both comfortably touch the ground on and pick up, so in theory, I should have been able to handle just about anything. Well, the bike could. My mind was still another story. But fortunately, I also now had a riding partner who let me lead, so I wouldn't end up alone and terrified and lost. There's a subtle confidence that comes from that. Hopefully that would make all the difference.

It was Carolanne's first time on a motorcycle, and my first time doing trails since the KLR debacle, so we started out easy. We hopped on the main fire road at a pace that would have even been too slow for Driving Miss Daisy, where deep ruts took my tires hostage. I was dragged along on squiggly rails, until we followed a sign for our first trail. None of us knew the area, but we had a map on our phones that colored the trail green for "beginners."

Perfect.

And it did seem rather green. We hooked around hills on a trail comfortably wide enough for a UTV. We were following an exposed cliff again, but the trail offered enough room that it didn't feel terribly daunting, and I had enough adventure riding experience under my belt now on my Alaska to Panama trip, that a wide road with a cliff was par for the course.

I'd tense a little when rocks would kick out my rear wheel, but I was able to recover time and again. The trail peaked, giving us 360 views of both Kremmling and the beautiful, vibrant blue reservoir below. We regrouped for trail snacks, and with everyone feeling enthusiastic, we decided to continue.

No one bothered to check the map, however, or we would have known that the trail difficulty jumped up to intermediate from there.

The dirt path immediately downturned, becoming increasingly rocky and increasingly steep. I practically locked my spongy rear drum brake as my bike skidded downwards. I feathered my clutch with desperation, trying to slow my momentum. It took very little speed to feel out of control, and every rock that deflected my front tire wasn't adding to my security. I chanted in my head a "you got this" mantra, until I made it to the last leg of the hill. Not more than thirty feet from the bottom, the dirt was spattered with all manner of jagged rocks, some tightly packed into the ground, others more in the form of loose shale.

As my mind rapidly processed the million ways I was about to crash, I made the always fatal mistake of stopping, killing the momentum that could have rolled over the obstacles without issue, and giving my brain that much more time to build stress and fear and anxiety. I rolled my bike to the side of the trail, so I wouldn't get ass packed by my riding companions, only to dismount and see... I was completely alone. No one ahead. No one behind. It was just me and this decidedly impassable hill.

I waited for a few moments, but still nothing. I'm pretty sure I didn't roll down the hill *that* fast. Certainly not at my nonexistent skill level. And there weren't multiple paths to take, so I know I didn't make a wrong turn for once. I paced around a bit. Crouched down with my camera so I could take some good pictures when everyone caught up, and I waited.

Aaaaand waited.

Where is everyone?!

I started to rock my bike back and forth to turn it around to make sure everyone was okay. Though its weight seemed much greater when being pushed up hill. I had half turned it around with a 500 point turn by the time Carolanne and Hollywood appeared over the crest of the highest hill. They rolled down past me with relative ease, and they settled in at the very bottom.

My face flattened as I stared at both the hill I was afraid of, and the bike that was now going to take even more muscling to turn around. Though after watching them both bumble down the hill, tires bouncing all over the place at not-so-in-control speeds, I wasn't feeling any better about riding that hill myself.

I hiked down those last thirty feet to discuss our options. The other side of this dip included an even steeper and longer hill, though the terrain was smoother, and it would be a climb rather than a drop, so I felt more confident in it. But Carolanne wasn't much enjoying either idea.

The reason they had taken so long to catch up was largely because her bike had stalled, and that hard starting CRF150R (that hadn't been properly tuned for the high elevation of the mountains yet) had taken a half marathon worth of kicking to get it to fire up again. She wasn't fond of hill climbs to begin with, but she figured if she stalled the high revving little race bike on the steep incline, it would be an accomplishment and a half to get it going again.

By my equally nervous calculations, it was a reasonable hesitation.

So instead, we opted to turn around. Two of this three person group were dirt bike beginners, and Hollywood didn't mind if we called the shots. Even if he made sure to remind me that I was a pussy before we headed out.

Carolanne took off first, accidentally popping the clutch and nearly wheeling into a fence to start. But some combination of luck and instinct brought the wheel back down, and she braaaped all the way back up the hill.

I, on the other hand, stared at my bike, stared at the hill, and then sat down on the fence to take a breather. It shouldn't have been that hard, but I felt completely overwhelmed. Had I already found the limits of my ability? On this silly little rocky hill?

No matter how frustrating that concept may have been, my desire to do better didn't erase my desire to cry. I took a ten count (Okay more like a thirty count), then climbed back up to my bike and finished turning it around. I shrunk into the weeds as some other riders buzzed by. Most popped up the hill without a moment's hesitation. Another stalled beside me.

"Sorry, first day on a dirt bike." He said to me with a tip of his visor. Then he kicked his bike back to life and powered up the hill with a smile on his face.

He had come from a far more technical side of the trail, including the steep ascent that had us turning around, and yet he didn't have any issues or fear at all?

Why was I so broken? Why couldn't I be like that? My self-preservation became even more annoying as the proud beginners buzzed me. I had long accepted that some people are more natural on a dirt bike than I am, but it never helped my confidence to be the one person who didn't get it.

It was with an even bigger sigh that I threw my leg over the bike. Hollywood waited for me to go first, just in case I needed his help. I knew I had no choice but to figure it out, so I took a deep, long held breath, and I took off up the hill.

For some reason, hill climbs are much easier for me mentally than descents. That little tractor of a bike rolled right over everything, and it climbed that hill without letting its inexperienced rider drag it downward. We regrouped with Carolanne at the top and followed the trail back to the truck.

I had nearly forgot the trauma of it all once we were back in green-circle pastures, and I even did a few laps around the parking lot to get in some extra riding and practice. It was a solid first outing, I guess. I felt better once I was getting out of my sweaty gear, alive and unharmed. But, despite any debatable success I had, I couldn't help leaving that day feeling like maybe dirt bikes *still* just weren't for me.

Try as I might, it was more scary than it ever was fun. And my own insecurity and inability only made me less eager to learn.

But there was nothing else to do in COVID times, so I would just keep hammering at it, I suppose. It had to get easier eventually, right?

My first dirt bike experience was about as awkward as you might expect anything involving me to be. Unfortunately, I gave up on it fairly quickly as a result. Second time's a charm? (Gorman OHV Park, California)

Laughing or crying? If I'm riding in the dirt, it could go either way. (Kremmling, Colorado)

I swear it felt more extreme than it looks in pictures. (Kremmling, Colorado)

When Hollywood and Carolanne finally showed up, I was relieved that no one was hurt… But also that I didn't have to go back alone to find them. (Kremmling, Colorado)

The epic views are the one thing that make me want to keep trying to learn to ride one of these wild things. (Kremmling Colorado)

Carolanne was our trusty navigator. And by trusty, I meant she led us into the abyss. (Kremmling, Colorado)

Chapter 3

It was another week before we returned to Kremmling. I was nervous but hopeful that a second trek would work out in a way that was a bit more confidence inspiring than the last outing. At the very least, I had some idea of what to expect of the terrain, and I had a one-for-one record of not dying, so I had some reason to bring confidence to the plate.

It's a conflicting feeling to be hungry to learn, but so intimidated by the sport that you're more afraid than excited to actually go through the process. I was reacting to dirt bike riding like a scared shelter dog, cowering in the corner of my kennel from the hand trying to feed me treats. I wanted those treats. Really, I did. But did that hand belong to a friend? Or was that hand going to highside me to the moon?

It was still impossible to say at this point.

This time, Dennis was in town, so he dusted off his KTM 250 that he ordinarily used for motocross. It was a bit worse for wear, with a broken starter that required the bike be push started any time he wanted to get it going. For such a great mechanic, it was almost comical to see his personal bikes in such disarray, but as Carolanne had put it, it was like "the shoemakers shoes," where he was so caught up making sure everyone else had perfect things, that his own equipment was forgotten in the interim.

It was an easily relatable concept, as I often did that to myself when it came to self-care. That "everyone's needs before my own, and I'll make due with what's left" mentality was deeply ingrained in me by a lifetime with an excess of empathy and a deficit of self-esteem, and I was still having to very consciously fight against it.

35

But unlike my ability to navigate healthy and unhealthy relationships, his bike problems were a fairly minor inconvenience. He gave it a push, the bike roared to life, and it was time to commit to the ride.

Determined to make it all the way down to Wolford Reservoir this time, preferably in a spot where we could take a swim on this warm, early summer day, we opted for the same loop as the first time. But not feeling confident that I was going to make it through that pair of hills with any more success, we also opted to do it backwards. It was a trail wide enough for two way traffic, so there was no reason to limit ourselves to a single direction. And hell, maybe the back end of the trail would actually be easier.

Like just about all of my bright ideas, I was wildly wrong.

The trail started with a long sloping uphill, with uneven mounds and deep crevasses shaped by erosion. My line snaked back and forth to find the easiest transitions between each mound, never feeling terribly confident that I wouldn't catch a rut just wrong and go tumbling over the bars.

I made it to the top by holding my breath long enough that I was a natural airbag, then I made it through the next portion of simple fire road switchbacks with a slow exhale. Dennis, being bored and disinterested in our low-level learning, romped about off the trail, jumping stumps and rocks and shrubbery. He rode literal circles around us, while I was doing my best to ignore the buzzing orange machine pestering my peripheral vision.

Fortunately, the trail demanded my attention as it turned into a tour of all that Kremmling had to offer. The desert gravel gave way to dark, reddish brown soil, shaded by an unexpected patch of pine. I smashed my rear break with an ogre's finesse, as the trail turned downward over large roots and eroded holes. I forced my eyes on the portions of the road that I actually wanted my wheels to travel over, relying on the age old adage to "look where you want to go," but my field of vision couldn't help peering into the pits that plunged into some unknown realm.

I made it down on luck alone, but I made it. I would have given myself a high five and a pat on the back if the trail didn't decide to puke a bunch of loose shale all over the place.

My tires slipped and slid in a way that was very much not Tiff approved. My rear brake that I held locked in a panic did little to aid with traction. After a couple hundred feet, I was about ready to just walk my bike down. Hell, I was dabbing so much, I may as well have been walking it already.

I acknowledge that not wanting my tires to slide on a dirt bike is like taking up swimming and not wanting to get wet, but fear doesn't use logic. Choosing a two wheeled vehicle that's very existence is a constant fight with gravity then riding it in wildly uneven terrain doesn't exactly scream logic either.

At one point, Carolanne got her first crash out of the way, with a mild, near zero mile per hour drop. All of my prior dirt bike escapades had already involved enough crashing, so I let her have the honors that day. It would have been selfish to eat all the shit.

Then, by some combination of white knuckles and letting Jesus take the handlebars, we arrived at the shore of the reservoir.

Leading up to this moment, on this warm and exhausting day, I had envisioned arriving at the lake shore and immediately stripping out of my gear, tossing my jacket to the wind, and diving head first into a revitalizing oasis.

Reality, however, had me staring, bewildered, at the dried overgrowth that stood between us and about 15 feet of brown sludge and muck. My standards are low, but they ain't that low.

So instead, we just parked the bikes for a break and a snack. Water tastes incredible when you're covered in sweat and coming down from the stress of a beautiful Sunday on your death machine.

From there, the ride took us back to the loop we'd been riding the day before. Somehow, after surviving the shale garden and eating some snacks, I found myself feeling pumped and riding unusually confident. I led the group through the trails, until we arrived at the crest of the hill that had turned us around the week prior. The hill was as steep and long as I remembered, but this side was smooth and free of daunting obstacles. I didn't give myself time to second guess myself as I modulated my weak ass drum brakes, making my best effort to keep myself one notch below completely out of control speeds. At the bottom was an upward slope that would act as natural brakes to slow me down, which meant there was no risk of barreling into the bending fence up ahead. The image in my mind's eye saw little to fear in this too fast descent.

The G forces compacted then released as my bike touched the bottom of the hill, then it continued its momentum over the following hump. Satisfied, I parked my bike next to the fence I had been borderline crying on the week before, and I waited for the rest of the team.

Carolanne wasn't feeling the drop, so she opted to walk her bike down. The CRF150R is technically a high revving MX bike and not a trail bike at all, so it lacked the low speed tractor gears of my KLX125. As such, in a

38

downhill situation, it was bound to hit much more intimidating speeds if left to its own devices. Not feeling ready for that kind of commitment, she put the bike in gear, and used a combination of the clutch and brakes to get herself all the way down.

Balancing the weight of a motorcycle while also balancing stiff dirt bike boots on a downhill hike was something far beyond my walking ability, but sometimes making a task more physically difficult is preferable to dealing with the mental extremes. If I had to choose, I'd favor conserving my mind over my matter every time.

At the bottom, we were also confronted with the long rocky hill from the day before, but as both Carolanne and I had successfully conquered this hill already, it barely registered in my mind. My anxiety was funny like that. The unknowns were near insurmountable, but the second they became knowns, they were basically laughable.

I used this repeat event as an opportunity to focus on how I used my vision, trying to force my target fixation on the path I actually wanted to ride, while forcing the scariest rocks and ruts into my periphery. I made my best attempt to keep my feet on the pegs when crossing the worst of the obstacles, but well, we'll just say that's still a work in progress. We're still only on the second baby step right now.

By the time we got back to the truck, I had all but completely forgotten the mild trauma of the beginning of the ride. To say I was loving dirt bikes was still a bit of an exaggeration, but I was averaging a 9 on the stress scale instead of 10, which is all I could ask for at that point.

But I will say that it was helping a tremendous amount having someone like Carolanne along for the ride to learn with. Where I struggled, she would push on, showing me that even a beginner could manage the obstacles safely. And where she struggled, I felt compelled to step up as her example. If it could be called competitive, it was in a gentle and good natured way that motivated us both to challenge ourselves just a little more, without having to feel ashamed if we made a mistake. The more I rode with her, the more I realized that this was a dynamic that I legitimately needed to improve more easily.

It was similar to my beginnings with road racing, really. I had been doing track days (open lapping days used for practice, without any form of timed competition) for a couple years before I got my race license. I had found myself stagnating at a fast C group (The beginner group), slow B group (The intermediate group) pace, and I didn't have the confidence to fully commit to bumping up to the faster group. So when my friends urged me to try racing, I was even more tentative.

But I was riding a little Ninja 250, and the local race series offered a 250cc class, so if anything, it would actually be a safer place to grow than being on track with dramatically different machines, high speed differentials, and unpredictable riding abilities. A race environment had a way of weeding out the totally unsafe beginners, and it demanded a certain standard from its entrants.

When I lined up for the first time on that grid, butterflies in my stomach and strangers who would soon be good friends on either side of me, my mind was filled with doubt.

My front tire was firmly planted on the white line of my grid spot. A harmony of increasing revs filled the air. The green flag dropped, I dumped the clutch, and the chase was on.

Knowing I was surrounded by like bikes of the same power and turning ability, I found myself pushing harder than ever. If he could take a corner that fast, so could I. If she could get that much drive off the apex and brake that hard into the next turn, my bike could, too. The person in front of me became a carrot that I wanted to both catch and toss behind me.

We call this "Red Mist" in racing, where you let your drive to pass the person in front of you override your usual survival instincts that over think how deeply you can brake into a turn or how fast you can accelerate out of it. You function on desire instead of logic, and you trust your muscle memory and sight line to get you through each corner safely.

Again and again, your brain processes the thought "if they can do it, so can I," until you're moving seconds faster than you knew was possible.

But this only works if there are other riders somewhere near your level—slightly better, perhaps (or maybe only slightly better in certain corners), but not completely outclassing you in every way, shape, and form. If a beginner hops on the track with Valentino Rossi, for example, the difference in skill would be so vast, and his ability would seem so unobtainable, that trying to chase him down would be pointless. That pro rider has a lifetime of finesse and knowledge and small nuances to his movements that would be impossible to emulate with my still clumsy, unskilled hands. Trying to match his speed would put me on my ass so fast, I wouldn't even want to ride motorcycles anymore. And more significantly, I'm *aware* of this gap in skill.

While Rossi is an extreme example, riding with Hollywood all the time felt similar to the concept of just being so outclassed that I never felt like I should even attempt the things he claimed were so incredibly easy. While I was trying to get used to riding a dirt bike at the age of 32, he had already been riding one for nearly that many years.

Hollywood's background was fairly typical in that regard. Like most kids who grew up in the country (or anywhere less ghetto than where I grew up), he learned to ride a bicycle not long after learning to walk, which incidentally gives you crucial motor skills that help a lot in future two wheeled endeavors. He then had the opportunity to fool around on dirt bikes with the neighborhood kids as he got older.

But his real experience with bikes came when he was about twelve. Once he moved from Montana to Colorado, he was working on a ranch in Steamboat Springs over his summers, and at some point, he made a deal with a farmer to trade some labor for a 1978 Suzuki RM125. The bike wasn't running due to a bent piston, I'm told, but nothing a hammer and some farm shit couldn't fix. From then on, he rode as much as he could, paving new trails over the hills and pastures of Steamboat Springs. Learning all of his skills and making all of his mistake before his brain could register consequences (I'm still not sure if it does), helps a lot with the early growing pains of a new skill. I can't imagine the freedom of being able to make careless decisions without having to worry about being bankrupt by the US medical care industry, or about bones and ligaments not healing properly.

Being a better rider wouldn't have been a big deal at all if not for the fact that Hollywood couldn't understand or relate to any of my mental hang ups, and he seemed to honest to god *believe* that telling me to "stop being a pussy" was going to make me suddenly feel comfortable fucking sending it.

By contrast, Carolanne was a similarly reasonable and careful adult with a similar desire to not die or get hurt, so we were able to play off each other and set limits to what was reasonable at our current level. We pushed each other with small shoves instead of throwing each other off cliffs, and Hollywood seemed to learn small amounts of patience when he found himself outnumbered.

Playing off of her became an integral part of my overcoming the bumps and fears. I felt as if I had evolved from "three legged newborn deer wearing roller blades" to something like "an octopus trying to ride a bicycle in a rock garden." One day, I hope to make it to "a human who is mildly okay at dirt bikes" level, but that might take a few hundred more tries.

We returned to Dennis and Carolanne's guest room in Silverthorne, and my moderate success had me fired up to get some more riding in. I felt for the first time in a while I had found real progress, and I wanted to keep it going. Every day not on the bike was a day my skills might start to relapse, so it was important to keep momentum going. Conveniently, Dennis was also on the "doesn't have a job" train, ever since his mechanic shop was sold, so on a beautiful Wednesday, we decided to try our hand at Tiger Road in Breckenridge.

North Fork was to be the trail of the day. Carolanne warned me before she left for work that it would be rocky, but after the hill in Kremmling, I thought I knew what that meant.

Ah, the naiveté of youth.

Like Hollywood, Dennis was a much better rider than I was. While all of us were more about the road racing scene than the off road scene, unlike myself, they both had an abundance of experience in the latter despite. It probably helped in both of their cases that, as racer dudes so often do, they both had that easy [over]confidence that had no

43

issue hopping on any given bike and not caring about whether or not they die in the process.

I've always envied that ability: to not over think things. Or maybe it's more than that. It was the ability to completely, shamelessly, and without question trust in your own ability. Whether it was because of ego, skill, or misguided stupidity, at its very core, it was an extreme form of self-confidence and self-esteem. Despite all of my little victories over the years, despite having raced motorcycles, traveled through foreign countries, and conquered high speeds and long distances on bikes, my mind and heart rate never genuinely trusted myself.

This is a struggle I expect to wrestle with my entire life though. So while I could let it crush me, as I continue to try to learn to ride a dirt bike, I'll fight that lack of confidence with pure internal spite.

Multi-million dollar vacation homes lined the smooth dirt road into the back country of Breckenridge, where we unloaded at the first pull out.

I was feeling capable as I threw my leg over the bike that day. So much so that I even hit fourth gear as we tore down Tiger Road to the first fork. We had already discussed our strategy and established my safe word—and by strategy I mean I made them both promise we could turn around if the trail was too much for me, and by safe word I mean they promised to actual listen. Light ruts and ripples opened the North Fork trail, a road that was more than wide enough for a trophy truck. In no time, the ruts turned to the occasional speckling of well seated rocks. In even less time, the trail could barely be found under all the rocks jutting out of the earth.

I dabbed so much, I could have been jogging. Either I picked all the worst lines (probable) or this trail needed far more substantial ground clearance than my 125 could manage (less probable). I was struggling, but at the very least, I was doing so at a rate that was so impossibly slow, it wasn't particularly dangerous. Gravity and terrain and my skill deficit all worked together to keep my bike at speed one notch above a stand still, and I clawed my way over rock garden after rock garden.

I can't say I was terribly afraid of continuing the climb. But the larger the stones and more abrupt the inclines, the more I started to worry about getting back down it. North Fork wasn't a loop, so every stone conquered uphill would have to be dropped off going downhill. The only thing I had going for me at this point was simply that the trail incline was more gradual than steep.

After a couple miles, I waved to take a break, hoping to discuss some of these concerns.

"Even though I'm getting up this, I really don't think I can get back down." I confessed between swigs of water. "I'm worried if we keep going, I'm going to be stuck up here and one of you will have to ride it out."

"This is easy, you'll be fine." Dennis assured me, in that way that someone who has no idea how not fine and not easy the trail actually was.

"Figure it out, Pussy." Hollywood added, in a way that has never helped any pussies figure it out.

"Ugh." I sighed, in a way that was completely defeated by my Neanderthal companions. Yet, I'm still just a girl who can't say no, so with tentative commitment, we continued on.

More rocks. More mini boulders. Some roots. Some mud.

To say Carolanne was right would be so obvious it's not even worth noting. But by what must have been the fiftieth stone covered hill, I about had it.

"This is impossible. Let's turn around." I pleaded.

"We're almost there." Hollywood argued.

"You said we could turn around if I felt like it was too much." I pushed again.

"This isn't too much. You're fine."

"It's too much."

"It's not."

The exchange continued in the same vein up until Dennis volunteered to scout ahead. They both rode on, while I enjoyed an extended water break. A good ten minutes later, they were back.

"It's like half a mile more. There's maybe one little puddle crossing, and that's it." Dennis noted.

"And there's an abandoned mine up there." Hollywood pitched.

I let out a sigh. I should have seen this coming. For my safe word to work, I had to be riding with people who knew what safe actually meant.

But if it was really only half a mile more, I could probably finish it. One little puddle wouldn't be so bad. And old mines are kind of cool. Discovering lost history was one of the appeals of dirt bike riding in the back country to me, so this might be a good excuse to get my amateur-archaeologist feet wet. Plus, if I went just half a mile more, I could say I finished North Fork, and I'll admit that I wanted that merit badge for my collection.

"Fine." I agreed with reluctance to yet again press on. I knew them both well enough to know they were probably lying about the distance (And they were definitely lying about the size of the puddle), but my own desire to not give up was starting to seep into my brain. My tenacity is both a blessing and a curse.

Up and up and over we continued. A half mile down the road, a dark pool of surely freezing water covered the trail ahead. It was impossible to tell how deep it was, but it extended at least a solid ten feet of the trail.

"Just a little puddle." I repeated in my head, to an appropriately mocking tone. I let Hollywood go first to be the Guinea pig.

He blasted through the water without fear, kicking up a large rooster tail on each side of the bike as he parted that puddle like the Red fucking Sea. Dennis went through next, with a touch less reckless abandon, but equal disruption. Then I swallowed my dread and went for it.

Thank god for Gore-Tex.

Fortunately, I had already learned the hard way how NOT to do a stream crossing back in Dinosaur National Monument, when I was touring through on my street bike—and more recently in Mexico where I learned that the desert has no drainage. I kept my throttle steady and true, making no sudden movements or abrupt inputs. The dirt below was smooth enough to cause no big disturbances, and the bike made it to the other side still on two wheels.

The trail kept on (for far longer than just a half mile, if anyone was wondering). Another stream crossing and another. My speed couldn't outrun a turtle with a broken leg, but I was putting on a solid slow race as my little bike continued to climb more and more and more rocks. Another mile, and at long last I found the obstacle that would stop me in my tracks.

A rocky creek bed covered the entire length of the trail, extending beyond my line of sight. The rocks would have been enough of an obstacle on their own, but at this time of year, the creek bed still had, well, a creek in it. That crystal clear water was flowing down the trail, a few inches deep and completely unencumbered.

I've crossed a few streams now, but I've never attempted to ride directly through one.

"You'll be fi—"

"Ice cream." I cut Hollywood off before he could finish the usual "you can do it" bullshit. "If I do this, you owe me ice cream."

I knew a place like Breckenridge was bound to have one of those fancy, hand-churned, gluten-free, organic, whatever-the-fuck ice creameries. And if I was going to keep suffering, I could at least do it with ice cream. Double points if it was chocolate and creamy and filled with nuts and hand-dipped peanut butter cups.

Hollywood smiled and gave me a pat on the shoulder. "Fair. If you don't quit, we'll go get ice cream after."

"Deal."

I spoke confidently, but let me tell you I was *not*. My tires slipped and dropped off every wet rock, while ice cold water splashed into the small holes in my well-used ADV gear. I made it half way through with a combination of luck and paddling, until a small waterfall finally stopped my impressively slow charge. I managed to propel the front tire over the smooth stone step up, but my rear tire just started digging. In a last ditch attempt of pushing and throttle modulation, I stalled the bike, and I was stuck. The stones acted like a wheel chock, propping up my bike by its rear tire. If nothing else, that made it easier to dismount, so I could free my poor little tractor the old fashioned way.

It took a lot of finagling, ending in Dennis helping me to physically lift the bike's wheel out of the rut to get it free, then it took about a thousand kicks to get my bike moving under its own power again. I suppose that's what happens when you're riding a bike jetted for sea level at over 10,000 feet.

But with thanks to my waterproof Alpinestars boots, I made it out of the fresh snowmelt without bringing any hypothermia with me. We finished our descent of the North Fork Trail without further ado. The only noteworthy event from here was the scenery.

Breckenridge is gorgeous. It's green, it's pine, it's dark rocks and quartz and fool's gold glittering in the cliffs. Remnants of log cabins from the gold rush miners still remained in the hillside, and the vibrant blue lupines sprung up wildly in the grass. My mouth fell open in a permanent smile as I witnessed this feat of beauty on the other side of all those feats of riding peril.

I guess this was worth the pain. It would definitely be worth the ice cream.

But at the top, snow still covered the trail. Testament to the Colorado altitudes, where weather is unpredictable even in May (which I can also attest to from the last time I came through Steamboat Springs in May and got snowed on. Or the time I road Trail Ridge Road in Rocky Mountain National Park and got caught in a mid-June blizzard. *Or* that time I was watching the Pikes Peak Hill Climb nearly in July and ALSO got snowed on. Snow and motorcycles and I have a tumultuous relationship). Though even if the weather hadn't been the final impasse, the legitimate end to the trail was. With nowhere else to go, we at long last turned around, and it was time to do the whole thing in reverse.

Much to my surprise, despite my internal assumptions that the trail was going to be impossible and death defying on the way down, the hills proved to be a gentle enough slope that I could easily stay in control of my bike by modulating the rear brake and trying to pick very careful lines. Rocks that seemed massive on the way up were mild inconveniences that were easy to dodge or roll over on the way down, and seeing the trail from the top (instead of looking up at it from below), was a perspective that gave me new confidence. The rocks looked smaller from this angle somehow, and the good lines were easier to pick out.

I still stalled the bike and got stuck in that stream again (probably in the rock pile I had built trying to unbury my wheel the first time), but the rest of the ride was both fun and only mildly challenging. I bumbled down past the hard parts, now used to the feeling of my rear wheel bouncing and my front tire deflecting, and I was going twice as fast in the easy parts. When the forest opened up into the wide open dirt of Tiger Road, I was standing on my tiny pegs and skidding back to the parking area on high.

I disrobed through my laughter (but quickly, because it was also starting to rain), and I knew in that moment that this was a genuine turning point in my dirt riding career. It was challenging enough to be far beyond anything I saw possible before, but enjoyable enough to have me yearning for more.

Admittedly, I was too pumped on adrenaline to even think about ice cream (which someone *still* owes me for this ride), but against all odds and awkwardness, I actually somehow had... *fun.*

Maybe I can do this dirt biking thing yet!

The thought of jumping in the lake at the other side of the trail was an enticing carrot to keep me motivated... even if the actual lake ended up being way too gross to actually enjoy when we got there (Kremmling, Colorado)

I'm pretty sure the phrase "stream crossing" is supposed to mean, I don't know, CROSSING the stream and not riding through it. (Breckenridge, Colorado)

One thing I'm quickly learning with dirt bikes, is that the scenery very strongly operates on the principles of "No pain, no gain." And let me tell you, this was a pain. (Breckenridge, Colorado)

Despite trying terrain, the only drop the whole day was Dennis's bike, when Hollywood buzzed him while his kickstand-less KTM was propped up against a tree branch. (Breckenridge, Colorado)

While I'll upgrade to real dirt bike gear eventually, this was one case where I didn't mind wearing my waterproof ADV gear. (Breckenridge, Colorado)

At nearly 12,000 feet, there's still snow in these mountains even in May. Which is why this was the end of the line. (Breckenridge, Colorado)

Chapter 4

If you don't like the weather in Colorado, wait 5 minutes.

I'd heard this a lot since coming to the state of many colors, and the "joke" certainly wasn't exaggerated. Even in the thick of summer, there was no way to predict whether the day would be sunny or frigid or under a torrential downpour. And my fourth attempt at not sucking at dirt bikes brought all of those things.

On what started out as a beautiful weekend, we opted to ride up around Snyder's Creek in Northern Colorado. Hollywood had been there before for trail clearing, and he was of the opinion that this trail circuit was both high in quality but also high in difficulty, so I was feeling somewhat tentative about the whole thing. Fortunately, Dennis and Carolanne volunteered to come along, so having at least one other beginner in the group, with two boyfriends who hopefully cared about said beginner's well-being (okay, maybe only one boyfriend who did), meant there would be some allowances for easier trails.

Though while Hollywood and Dennis perpetuated this claim that they totally cared about not scaring the bejeezus out of us, I wasn't sure what to expect from Hollywood's friend who we would be meeting there.

Chris was an incredibly experienced rider, and he was very well versed in the hundred-some miles of trails in Snyder Creek. He was an older gentleman who'd been riding motorcycles for a majority of his life, but like myself, he started out as a street rider whose need for speed brought him to a race track, where he primarily developed his riding skills. Also like me, dirt riding came much later in his life.

Though unlike me, after many years, many schools, and miles and miles and miles of some of the most advanced riding the western United States had to offer, he was at the level I could only hope to reach at some point in the next decade.

Excuse me if I was a little bit intimidated. I did my best to make it clear I was still very much an amateur, and I could only hope that my definition of amateur was at least somewhere near his expectations.

We parked in a wooded lot among a throng of other riders and unloaded in the grass. The high altitude and the cold morning reminded me exactly why I hated owning a vehicle that's carbureted. Doubly so when it's kick start only. The only advantage was that it was proving to be great physical therapy for the atrophied thigh muscles in my right leg, which had withered away after injuring my knee in a car accident the year prior.

Though as great as that was, I still could have done with a slightly less exhausting start to what I already knew would be a very long day.

Chris, likely tired of watching me struggle, demonstrated the "cold-starting-bitch" secret handshake, by pumping the kick starter at the top of the stroke a few times to build pressure. Then with one swift kick, the little eight horsepower motor chirped to life.

Carolanne's newly re-jetted CRF150R was a little bit more of a handful. A thousand hard kicks later, the guys eventually resorted to push starting it, in hopes of getting it to warm up and be a bit more pliable.

All geared up and with bikes mostly running, Chris waved us on to the trails.

Despite our insistence that we keep the ride nice and easy, reminding Chris that it was Carolanne's third time ever on a dirt bike, and that I was still a heap of nerves and self-doubt and shoddy technique, this day still started out with a bit of a baptism by fire.

We hadn't even made it 500 yards before we were rolling over a small log. Then another 100 yards and we were staring down our first ever stint of single track.

The trail was narrow and heavily recessed into the earth, as though someone had dug a half mile trench up a mountain and called it a motorcycle trail. My foot pegs were barely higher than the banks of the trail, and the trench was barely wider than the tires, so if I wanted to stop, I had to put my feet outward onto the banks.

"You know they're both still beginners," Dennis said with a flattened expression.

"This is only a few hundred feet, then it opens up," Chris replied as an appeal to unreasonable reason.

"I'll try it." I gave everyone a nod with a resolve that I couldn't quite explain. I must have been feeling confident after the last stint on North Fork, because this didn't seem nearly as daunting as it should have. It may be because the tall walls of the trail meant there was no possibility of falling to my doom, or maybe I was just in a rambunctious mood. But either way, I was game.

"Great." Chris sounded pleased. "Now as a warning, there's going to be a root up ahead. Just don't slow down and you'll be fine."

With that, he took off up the trail, checking back behind him every now and again to verify we were still there. I followed along, focusing on the line and not at all on what was going on behind me. A tunnel vision strategy I employed more because of a deficit of available attention, and less because of a disregard for the rest of my companions. My little KLX125 tractored right over

56

everything, including the substantial step up that had been sold as a simple root, and with only a mild stint of anxiety, I brought my bike to the two-track clearing at the top of the hill. I won't say I felt strong and confident or anything, but this was nothing compared to Breckenridge. The advantages of early learning trauma.

I parked next to Chris, and we looked back to see no one was behind us. Odd. Once again, I had barely out-sprinted a sloth, yet once again, I was alone on the trail.

Chris and I shrugged to each other.

"You wait here, and I'll go see what's up," Chris suggested. I certainly wasn't going to argue. I sipped on a water bottle and got comfortable as minute after minute passed. A pair of other riders passed by. Still no sign of the team. I'm not sure how it was even possible for those riders to have passed them by on such a deep and narrow rut of a trail. Someone must have jumped over something.

About the time I was starting to worry, at long last, I saw a flash of Hollywood's helmet poking through small clearings between the dense pine trees. As he braaaped around the banked single track like he was on rails, I saw that he wasn't on his Kawasaki 250, but Carolanne's bright red race bike.

Chris followed. Then Dennis. Then Hollywood hiked back down to get his own bike, while Carolanne hiked up to get hers.

Carolanne was visibly frustrated, and I couldn't blame her. Her bike had stalled on the trail and they had to roll it up the berm to clear the trail for other riders until they could get it started again. Hollywood and Dennis had tried to re-jet the carburetor the day prior in preparation for these high altitudes, but as carburetors continue to be extremely simplistic yet impossibly unpredictable motorcycle voodoo, they had clearly gotten it wrong. So to get thrown straight into a more advanced trail before the bike or the rider was warmed up, with an audience of other riders who you don't know, no less, was a recipe for injured confidence.

Once we got past the first single track section, we continued down a comfortable, tree-shaded two track that gave everyone easy comfort. Puddles of mud from freshly melted snow still speckled the trail, while fallen leaves blanketed the bumps and dips. It was a pleasant ride to the next spot of single track, where once again we were climbing over roots, set in a steep rut. I could hear Dennis groan in his helmet as he stopped in a clearing behind me, knowing this was everything they wanted to avoid.

I stared at the large rock on the skinny hill up ahead and let out a sigh myself. "So, remember when I said we didn't want to do anything too difficult?"

"I'm thinking Chris's definition of beginner friendly might be a little different from the beginners." Hollywood chimed in with a shake of his head.

Chris, who had gone ahead, hiked back down the trail. He dislodged the large rock with his boot and kicked it into the weeds.

"You've got this." He told me as he passed, heading down the trail to help out. I stared at the narrow climb and shrugged. It still felt easy compared to North Fork.

With a twist of the throttle, I covered the last few hundred yards to the top of the trail, and I parked and waited again. In a few moments, we had all regrouped, and Chris assured us it got easier from here.

I don't really know what "easy" means from a guy like Chris anymore, but so long as it didn't escalate beyond this, I was fairly certain I'd be fine. Fortunately, despite the challenges, Carolanne's resolve to continue hadn't wavered. She wasn't the type to be easily discouraged by a challenge. In hopes of wider pastures, we crossed the street to a new path.

And he was right this time. The next section was open and low consequence, allowing ample line choices to dodge any rocks, roots, or ruts. The trail climbed into the hills, while my wheels skipped over the small rocks and bounced up the loose stone washes. We ducked under dead aspens that were propped up by the surrounding trees, and we rolled over the fully fallen ones, whose six inch trunks shifted beneath our wheels. Further into the hills, pine cones created their own obstacle course, and further still, my bike snapped splintering branches that had been scattered by the wind. The road was tame enough that I likely could have even done it on my Yamaha FZ-07 with minimal bitching. On my dirt bike, I felt invincible.

I was fast. Well as fast as I knew how to go anyways. The tires rolled over everything without complaint. The suspension built for a child offered a few harsh words, but my traction didn't bat an eye as I splashed a tall wet roost through the stream crossings.

As my confidence grew, I even practiced standing up best I could on my awkwardly short bike. It didn't feel stable, and it certainly didn't appear to be helping much, as the miniscule proportions had me putting more weight on the bars than is prudent, but this easy road was a rare instance where I could at least try to practice better body position safely. I made sure to keep my elbows out as I soared around the mountainous turns.

Up at the top, we stopped for a bite. Though I think the mosquitoes managed far more nourishment than I did. I'm fairly certain the bird sized mosquitoes of the Northern United States were burly enough to bite directly through my armored jacket. We wasted no time beginning the descent.

The day had started sunny and lovely, but between the heavy tree cover and my focused joy, I hadn't noticed the threatening clouds that had rushed in overhead. Like the schizophrenic state that it is, the mountains of Colorado saw fit to start drizzling, which then saw fit to turn into a sudden icy hailstorm.

Having still not yet gotten any dirt bike specific gear, I was wearing my Gore-Tex adventure gear that I use for world travelling, so it was no bother to me. If anything, I felt even more badass as little balls of ice plunked in the flowing streams beneath my tires, while I was comfortably warm and dry.

White pellets bounced off my visor as I raced ahead, hoping I might catch some photos of my riding companions.

The sun came out as quickly as it had left, and we finished the trails with another stint of single track. But this time, thoroughly warmed up and riding on a high, I didn't bat an eye. On the contrary, when given two choices, I chose the harder path. The narrow road flowed through endless whoops, in between trees sometimes barely spaced enough to fit my handlebars. My knuckles tagged a few branches along the way, but the carbon fiber armor on my gloves paid it no mind.

I was giggling in my helmet as I squeezed my front end between two towering tree trunks. Since when was dirt riding so fun?

This ride had brought about a whole new perspective, and instead of stress, I was flowing and jiving and just feeling alive. It was the kind of joy I had felt when I had first started to get comfortable on a street bike over a decade ago, and it was something I didn't think I could feel while going 15 miles per hour on rough terrain. This confidence was coming on faster than I ever could have expected, and the gorgeous landscape of the Rockies only lured me in more eagerly.

As we rolled out to the road on the other side of this tiny trail, I parked alongside Carolanne who was hollering with excitement.

"Single track like that, I would do a hundred times." She said with a smile that was visible behind her helmet's chin bar. Adrenaline was flowing freely between us, which is likely why no one said no when Chris proposed the final challenge.

Camp was on the other side of the highway. But alternatively, we could cross what he professed would be the most challenging stint of single track yet.

We all forged ahead, rolling over the hump of highway, directly onto another narrow clearing in the trees. I found myself a little tripped up as we shimmied down a winding ledge. Heavy cliff exposure alongside the tire wide trail is one thing that gives me the heebie jeebies. But with some extra caution and using my foot as a feeler to keep my wheels true, I inched down to the creek below. Up ahead, Chris was parked in the middle of the trail. He raised a hand to signal for us to stop, then he waited with us, single file, while Dennis scouted the coming section, knowing it might be particularly problematic. It was barely a few minutes before he was back with a report.

Despite volunteers having recently cleared this trail just two weeks prior, a recent storm had felled some new trees, and a large, impassable log blocked the way. In the event that we could get the bikes up and over it, the continuing snow melt had created a stream crossing that was deep enough to swallow my bike whole.

As we debated how foolish and cocky we wanted to be, Chris offered some sage advice that has stuck with me ever since. Advice I consider often as I stare down some of the worst obstacles I encounter. With one foot on the ground, and the other resting on the footpeg of his KTM 250, he turned to us and he said:

"We've had an incredible day so far. If we go this way, it might be even more incredible. But it also might be so bad that it will ruin the entire day and all the confidence you've gained. So instead of risking injury and misfortune, let's turn around and revel in the successes we've already had."

Some might argue that's a lame outlook, dripping with entirely too much reason and not enough risk taking, but perhaps it's the self-preservation in me that thought "That makes perfect sense." It's not like we had taken no risks that day. It's not like we hadn't learned or developed skills.

Sometimes you need to know when to fold and save those obstacles for another time. So much of riding is mental, and this day I was finally feeling capable and proud. It would have been a travesty if I had any of that taken away from me while I was finally gaining momentum.

With some help from the guys, we all got our bikes pivoted back around. We climbed back up to the road and slabbed it on the asphalt until we got back to camp. I got off the bike, tired, beat, and completely thrilled.

What a day! What a ride! This is what motorcycling is supposed to be!

We stopped for ice cream on the way back that day, and that creamy chocolate frozen goodness had never tasted so magical.

I guess it counts as beginner friendly when the ravine is so deep, there's nowhere else for the beginners to go... (Snyder's Creek, Colorado)

This is more what I imagined when I heard the phrase "single track." Less steep, more squiggles through the forest. (Snyder's Creek, Colorado)

Dirt biking is definitely a hobby best shared with friends, both for learning and for the laughs. Having these guys along for the journey really made roads I thought were impossible feel much more possible. (Snyder's Creek, Colorado)

"So what were you saying about this being a nice easy day again?" (Snyder's Creek, Colorado)

I was riding so quickly and confidently, that I was actually able to get ahead of the group to take pictures for once! I'm starting to find that I love the drama and excitement of stream crossings more than any other obstacle. (Snyder's Creek, Colorado)

Chapter 5

After the last outing, we ended up taking a little bit of a break from dirt biking. I needed some time to catch up on my writing, finishing the first draft of a book about scuba diving in Southeast Asia, while Hollywood took the time to help Dennis catch up on some wrenching.

When the weekend came again, we all loaded up in our trucks for some four wheeled off roading, as we spent the day touring nearby abandoned mines in our pickup. Our tires climbed around the back roads and up into the mountains around Montezuma, Colorado.

The Pennsylvania Mine, which was settled into the hills behind Breckenridge, was once one of Colorado's biggest producers of gold back when it was founded in 1879. But now it was a toxic polluter, draining heavy metals into the nearby streams. Greed and nature rarely mix well, and these old mines often reflected that. Though that didn't take away my desire to climb around the century and a half old structures or to frolic with the abundant, and rather goofy looking, mountain goats.

The following week, we dipped over to Hollywood's parent's home in Loveland to help his dad install an engine into an old, bright orange 1967 Chevy Pickup. Hollywood was at home in the garage. He had always loved hotrods, having been raised around them. From his dad's drag racing to his own high school hooligan days, it was always such a nostalgic thing for him. His dad was still a passionate enthusiast, with something like eight different cars, ranging everywhere from the 1932 Buick with a straight eight to a 2020 mid-engine Corvette, with several thousand horsepower between the lot of them and their heavily modified, big block engines.

Though cars in general are a bit out of my own element. I knew how to work on one well enough to fix the little problems that came up when needed, like swapping brake pads or radiators or water pumps. But otherwise, I found cars to be too large, expensive, and difficult to work with without having an extensive shop and power tools. While I couldn't afford to not know how to fix things myself, I also couldn't afford to electively modify my grocery getters. However much we joke about the cost of a motorcycle racing addiction, it doesn't even scratch the tire budget of a car hobby.

Motorcycles were somehow much cheaper in their all-consuming allure. They only had two tires I had to replace after all, and a new exhaust or a power commander or even the rear shock and fork internals were all modifications that could be done with simple hand tools on a three figure budget.

I actually love working on bikes. It's therapeutic as long as things are going well, and the relative size and affordability makes it something anyone can do if they want to. It's empowering to have a vehicle that makes me feel capable and handy instead of powerless and poor. Well, not that there hasn't been plenty of trial and error in my wrenching career. I've stripped more bolts and screws than I can count (and as someone who took calculus for fun, I can count pretty damn high!), and I've even snapped a cam shaft when reinstalling the cams after a valve check on a 2009 Ninja 250.

But I've also *successfully* installed exhausts, suspension, clutches, and brake lines. I learned how to properly time the cams, how to extract stripped bolts, how to install and paint fairings, how to swap chains, sprockets, tires, and rework the ergonomics to build and modify my bikes to suit my size and preferences. Each failure and each success brought its own new confidence, and one by one, each "intimidating" job became accessible. In over a decade of wrenching on bikes, the only thing I can say I wouldn't ever choose to do again is, well, try to wrestle a stiff touring tire onto a sport bike rim with tire irons.

Just about everything I did for the first time was a little bit of a tight rope walk of clumsiness and success, but isn't that the case for everyone? That professional mechanic didn't learn how to fix things without failing a hundred times first. How can you know how to fix mistakes and broken things if you've never made them? Maybe the mechanic had the opportunity to make those mistakes when they were young, with a mentor to help, and when failure was more expected and accepted, but they still had growing pains just like I did, and they still had to build their own knowledge base just like I did.

This was something I needed to remind myself of when I started getting critical of my dirt bike riding ability. Every skill has a learning period, some longer than others. And it was okay to still be in the thick of it.

But for this week, I loved seeing Hollywood bond with his dad more, and it was a nice way for myself to get caught up on all the work I'd been putting off. I would set up my laptop in the shop, where the relaxing hum of air compressors and power tools would keep my mind focused, while Hollywood and his dad would run about with wrenches and welding torches as they tried to shove an engine that was entirely too large onto engine mounts that were entirely too small.

Though after over two weeks off the bike, I was starting to worry I might lose the small amount of momentum I had gained. And after a month or so of stagnating in Colorado, I was starting to feel nearly as trapped and stuck as I had felt at the beginning of the COVID lock downs. The depression of my ruined trip still nagged at the back of my mind, and the longer we sat still, the more desperate to move I felt. Colorado had been a great place to learn, but it was about time we got moving again.

But not without taking the test first. This is a boot camp after all.

To prove I was now fully committed to this dirt escapade, we first set our sights on getting outfitted with some new gear. As much as I liked my ADV gear, as we moved more into summer, I was sure I'd want something a bit less warm. And I would feel much more confident with full body armor, instead of just the shoulder, knee, and elbow armor that my set up provided.

We stopped in at the biggest gear shop in Denver, and like children in a candy store with a blank check, we spent literal hours trying on every piece of armor and combination of jersey colors we could get our hands on. None of the armor was female specific, so I settled for men's gear with a single piece chest plate that was snug enough to not be displaced by my squishy lady bumps, and some armored shorts that didn't have uncomfortable padding in places that I didn't particularly need. We scored a set of helmets that were half price due to having last-year's-paint, and I found some clearance jerseys in an eye catching teal. The fact that dark purple and teal was somehow in the men's section, while everything in the women's section was decorated exclusively with splashes of hot pink, is an injustice I can't even begin to address in something as short as a novel.

I decided to stick with my street boots, as they were more than capable of keeping me protected. Hollywood also continued running his adventure boots, so we didn't need any investment there. We left with a nearly $2000 hole in our pocket, which was still cheaper than the deductible would have been on the health insurance I neither had nor could afford (yay America!). With two fully outfitted riders, we were officially not turning back. We hit up Carolanne and planned our last ride in the state.

Dennis was once again out of town for road racing, but Carolanne had both local knowledge and local friends in the area who had no problem giving us some riding recommendations.

We opted into one last trip through Breckenridge with a ride that would be a culmination of everything I had learned.

We loaded up both trucks and hauled out to Tiger Road bright and early enough to hopefully miss the afternoon thunderstorms that seemed to roll in like clockwork, even on this lovely summer day.

We inched a bit closer to the possibility when we unloaded, only to discover that Carolanne had forgotten her boots at home. My scatterbrained ways might be rubbing off on my friends a bit more than I realized.

It reminded me of that time I had signed up for a six hour endurance race with some of my lady racer friends, and on one of our practice days, I made it 2 hours of the 2 ½ hour drive to the track when I realized my back protector wasn't in my suit where it should be.

But what can you do. Broken bones take way longer to heal than a couple hours, and I'd rather lose the time to driving back home than to recovery. So when we're talking something as critical as boots, we insisted that she go back for them instead of trying to improvise.

I waited with Hollywood, awkwardly modeling my shiny, new, pro looking gear with my child's bike, then a half hour later, she was already back and gearing up.

Carolanne loaded up her map, and we decided to go explore some new territory.

Tiger Road, incidentally, has a relatively extensive system of trails to choose from, ranging from wide to narrow, from simple to complex. I was feeling bold after our ride with Chris, especially knowing I had already conquered North Fork, so I didn't hesitate at all as the smooth dirt road turned to ascending hills of rocks.

Our ride climbed to old mining camps, where we parked and explored on foot, then to mountain tops where we could gaze upon the distant ski mountain, whose previously snowy runs were now covered in the greenest grass and the most colorful wild flowers.

Carolanne and I were both riding with a new confidence, not stumbling nor stopping even when the terrain threatened steep grade or high consequence. On the contrary, I barely noticed the consequence until I was reviewing go pro videos later. We carved down the hills with unusual speed, then splashed through puddles, flinging up chunks of mud from our rear tires wherever the shade of pine trees had kept the earth damp and full of good traction.

I felt like a dirt bike rider now. I was wearing the colorful jerseys, I was spinning my knobby tires, and I was actively electing to meet my friends at hairy, uncertain trails under the pretext of having *fun*. My bike was listening to me, getting me over roots and rocks and hills without issue, and the high fives and enthusiasm of both Hollywood and Carolanne, as we conquered one obstacle after the next, left me feeling like a rock star.

As the day wore on and the miles ticked away beneath our knobs, Carolanne glanced at her map, then she nodded toward a wooden arrow that pointed down some single track that would connect our trails to the parking lot.

It was one of those shortcuts that was neither short, nor did it cut much of anything. If the trail Chris had taken us to was a trial by fire, this was climbing out of an erupting volcano. Uphill, downhill, tight turns, tall step ups, and the most wild roots I'd ever seen. I stalled my bike while bottoming on a root that had created a tall drop off where the earth had eroded away around it. After dismounting, rolling the bike into stable ground, and trying for several minutes to get it to fire again, Hollywood took over and kicked it to life on his first try.

I still don't win them all, it seems. But that's what friends are for.

Our wheels just kept rolling, opting into a couple more single track diversions that added a few more miles to our loop. The only thing louder than our exhaust notes were our giggles.

When our short cuts finally spit us out on the clearing back to Tiger Road, we found ourselves facing one last obstacle.

A wide creek crossing flowed quickly over the rocks, rushing by at a rate that created white caps in the otherwise crystal clear water. It should have been an intimidating obstacle. We should have stopped to assess an easier way through. But for some reason, not one of us hesitated.

We plowed through the water, one at a time, getting an ice cold rush of adrenaline. My tire bounced around on the slick rocks, while my pants were dampened by snow melt. A refreshing end to a physically taxing ride.

We came barreling back to the truck just in time to beat the first spits of rain drops, and we loaded up quickly with permanent grins on our faces.

I left feeling confident I could do just about anything on my little bike. The KLX125 was a champion of terrain, and I was its master. I hadn't felt this empowered on a motorcycle since I had done my first track day. In my mind, I was almost a good rider now. I was learning and taking the right steps and this previously impossible task was now something I was proven capable of doing. And something I was actually enjoying.

There's a lot of satisfaction in that.

It might seem silly to have so much of my self-worth leaning on my ability to ride a motorcycle, but as someone whose spent a third of their life completely revolving around this sport, that's what I had. I bonded with people over learning, improving, and conquering new challenges, and I measured myself against other's ability to do the same. From the first time I put a pencil to paper to sketch my favorite comic book characters, I've been fiercely obsessed with my own self-improvement, and my hardcore nerd tendencies only amplified this with motorcycles, where I had a quantifiable way to determine how far I'd come.

For all intents and purposes, riding was like a leveling system in a video game for me, and this was how I leveled up, one experience point at a time. I equipped new armor, and I learned new magic spells and techniques.

Motorcycles are game-ification of life.

We loaded everything we had into the Chevy the following morning, and we said our latest goodbyes to our Colorado friends. As soon as we were on the highway, I made an unexpectedly bold request. Feeling unjustly invincible, I suggested our next stop be the northern Colorado Sand Dunes.

Hollywood was surprised but pleased. He had always wanted me to love dirt riding at least a fraction as much as he did, and for me to ask to go ride in the sand by choice was a degree of dirty bike excitement he hadn't thought me capable of.

There was no argument or question, as he turned off toward the dunes outside Walden, Colorado.

We meet again, my old nemesis.

Though the dunes in this region aren't really sand at all. The grains that cover the miles and miles of trails are crafted more by fine silt blown in by the always exciting wind in the mountainous valleys, which is somehow even worse than the coarse, grainy erosion built sand of Southern California or Mexico.

Let's just say this little side trip was a rodeo and a half. My knobbie tires clawed for traction with wild abandon, while sliding around like a dog wearing socks on freshly waxed linoleum. There's no such thing as a straight line in the sand. There's no such thing as control. And it turns out, 8 horsepower is more than enough to sink a tire into the earth deeply enough that you have to get on your knees and dig.

I think I walked my bike more than I rode it.

While this was a debatable life choice, I felt a little better when even Hollywood was struggling in the powder. Seeing someone who made everything look easy finally saying something was hard put it into perspective enough that this sudden barrage of failing didn't cause any backwards momentum in my always delicate confidence. Not the least of which because, while I'm still laughably bad at the sand, I kept it upright even on hills. In another 20 years or so, I totally have a chance of being 1% okay at this.

Maybe.

Not every battle can be a victory, so with a shrug of my shoulders, we continued north to the Wyoming line. New challenges await!

All dressed up with nowhere to go: A "My riding buddy forgot their boots" story. (Breckenridge Colorado)

Let's go, let's go, let's go! Hollywood was pleasantly surprised to see the ladies being enthusiastic and excited to try harder and harder trails. (Breckenridge Colorado)

During summer months, the ski mountains of Breckenridge are used for downhill mountain biking. Going down a steep, tree covered hill really fast on skinny tires is the extreme sport where I draw the line. (Breckenridge Colorado)

Found a nice fixer-upper. Probably end up in a bidding war to 4.5 million in this neck of the woods. (Breckenridge Colorado)

Our last ride with Carolanne was an epic one. I'm going to miss Colorado! (Breckenridge Colorado)

My relationship with sand has not improved. (Walden, Colorado)

Hollywood struggled in the fine silt, too. But every time I got a picture, he was in the middle of a brief stint of making it look easy. (Walden, Colorado)

Chapter 6

The wheels of our pickup rolled over the Colorado state line, placing us firmly in Wyoming. Immediately, my cell phone coverage shifted from 4G to Roaming, as if we had crossed into a foreign country. Seemed like a reasonable assessment of Wyoming.

It was a long drive to Dubois (Or Dubious, as Hollywood liked to call it. Or Du-Boys, as the locals preferred), and we'd already blown half the day on my fanciful need to face plant in the sand. While we could have driven late into the night, it made more sense to break up the drive. I located Medicine Bow National Forest on the map, the nearest patch of green public land where there would surely be plenty of free dispersed camping, and we began following the long road to Turpin Reservoir. A few wrong turns later, in increasingly ravaged and rain damaged roads, we stopped to ask directions. We came across an entire family of six, all piled onto the same ATV, who had fewer teeth than they had children among them, and they pointed us in the opposite direction we were going.

Back on track, the drive in was long and rough in our beat up old truck. Washboards rattled the cab, while our hefty tires ejected gravel behind us. I'd have insisted we stop sooner just so I didn't have to keep rattling my bones so hard, but every half way decent camping spot was already occupied by other campers. It didn't matter how obscure the spot or how deep in the mountains you thought you were—there were always people around now. It was as though the pandemic was the pied piper, leading the people from their comfortable cities into the unknown wilderness.

We continued past charred remnants of forest fires and fallen trees, over rocks, under branches, and through small stream crossings until we arrived at the reservoir. The lake was crowded too, but having been on the road for hours now, we were both tired enough to call it a night even if it meant being tent to tent with other campers. Every park-able surface was occupied by multiple rigs with multiple ATVs and UTVs and Side-by-Sides. It might have been annoying if it wasn't a fairly consistent thing nowadays. Everyone being unemployed, yet also making more money than I ever made while working full time in the tech industry, had driven consumerism in ridiculous directions. People who didn't know how to manage small amounts of money were now using big amounts of money to wrack up all the debt they could, buying brand new vehicles and leveraging their unemployment to the hilt, with no mind for what would happen once they were back to their old unlivable wages.

    The reason I was able to go on the adventures I did was because I'd always been taught to budget obsessively, to live below my means, and avoid debt whenever possible. All of my vehicles were ones that I saved up for and bought outright, that I learned to repair myself to save money when they broke down, and that I could afford to register and insure. I had discount clothing and didn't bother to collect things that had no function beyond being a status symbol. Even when I was road racing motorcycles, I picked the cheapest possible bike, budgeted for the longest lasting tires that still performed well, and I pinched pennies obsessively, clipping coupons and sacrificing nights out and the most organic produce so I could afford to save for a rainy day while still enjoying life. It was a fine dance of sacrifice and selective indulgence.

    Which I learned as an adult is very much not the American way. Rolex watches and Mercedes SUVs and $50 cotton T-shirts, all for the hope of appearing to have kept up with the Joneses, is the American way, and the pandemic was amplifying that to new extremes. This blissfully ignorant shirking of consequences to get the newest, shiniest, and most unnecessary diesel truck, the fanciest fifth wheel toy hauler, and the highest performance UTV, knowing it would likely get repossessed by the tax man as soon as that falsely inflated income tanked again? That was as American as our culture gets, honestly. Even our medical system is designed to throw people in debtor's prison, so how could I be surprised that aid for the pandemic threw everyone into a financially self-destructive frenzy.

But then again, on the flip side of that argument, when shut downs and quarantine and joblessness means you're not allowed to do anything that keeps you occupied, happy, or content—what else are you going to do?

That's why we were here, after all. Everything we valued had been ripped out from under us, and the idea of squandering an entire year of our short human lives with nothing that furthered our skills or happiness was so inconceivable to me, that I was willing to commit to a form of motorcycle riding that I previously hated just to prevent wasted time. I wasn't going to be going into massive debt to enjoy life, mind you, though I was a bit envious of all the people who were making money by fucking off, while we were only spending our savings. But ultimately, the motivation to be outside and exploring the wilderness was the same.

Philosophical disagreements aside, these people ended up being the least of our disruptions to what should have been a pleasant night.

Because as we settled in beside that calm lake water, now we were in the world of mosquitoes. In this world of mosquitoes, I'm something of a fine tiramisu. I'm delicious, soft, and easy to sink your teeth into, no matter how many layers I have, and that little bit of caffeine in the middle gives just enough energy to keep you hyped and ready for more. Apparently, standing at this gate to hell that had been unfairly disguised as a lake in Wyoming, I was so delicious, that not even a liberal spattering of 99% DEET was enough to make those mosquitoes slow their roll. It was like I had mixed them a cocktail made with Mexican water, and they tauntingly stared Montezuma in the eye as they chugged every drop.

When not a single of those vampire bugs were deterred by even the vilest, most plastic melting, cancer inducing poison I could wear, I found myself scrambling for the truck in a desperate bid to not be eaten alive. A gaggle of them made it inside with me before we could both get in and shut the doors.

They're evolving, I thought, while desperately rubbing more worthless DEET on my arms. Either that, or Wyoming really was another planet and this was a whole new species of fuck-you-bugs.

I swatted and smashed every stray flier that I could, but the barrage never seemed to end. I winced at the already swelling bumps on my skin as we fired up the truck and headed to the hills, hopefully far enough away to escape the hordes.

The next spot initially seemed a little better. The swarms were sparse enough that Hollywood was able to get a smoky fire going using the fresh leaves of a newly downed tree, and I was able to set up the tent under the protection of the blackened air. For once, I was thankful that the campfire smoke always seemed to be wafting in my direction.

But it was short lived respite. As the sun dipped below the clouds and we arrived at the witching hour—that moment at dusk where all of the wild animals suddenly decide to dart across the street, and all the world's bugs wake up hungry for their first meal—any hope we had of a nice night were destroyed. As their numbers sky rocketed, the smoke wasn't enough to scare the skeeters away anymore. It came to the point that even Hollywood had had enough (And mosquitoes don't even like Hollywood).

Once again, we were huddled in the truck, swatting bugs until we were down to rare stragglers. The underbody of mosquitoes filled my vision, as tens of hundreds landed on the windows, the windshield, and the still warm hood of the truck, every single hell gnat laying eagerly in wait for us to make our first mistake.

But while my layers and DEET did nothing to protect me, the thick glass certainly did. Once we had killed off the last of them inside, we both relaxed in the truck seats that had been our home for what seemed like so long now. I put on an audiobook, lit a citronella incense in hopes of warding off any remainders, and drifted off to sleep.

We gave up on any idea we had of riding our bikes in Medicine Bow. I don't think I would have survived stripping down and changing into my gear in these bug blackened skies. Stopping long enough to kick start the KLX was sure to be even more perilous. And those scenarios would all come AFTER being sitting ducks as we unloaded the truck.

Nope, nope, nope.

We didn't leave the truck again until the next morning, and only because I quite grudgingly had to break down the tent I thought we would get to sleep in. I didn't take the time to roll up or repack any of our camping equipment. I swatted mosquitoes off my face, while breaking down the tent in record time, multi-tasking with pure desperation.

With a half collapsed tent and partially inflated air mattresses in the back seat, we slammed the doors on the pickup (to be fair, it's old and we always have to slam the doors), and peeled out of camp. Hollywood drove, while I continued my campaign to kill off all the bugs that made it inside before I could shut the door.

Then, with a deep exhale, we were back on track.

Not the most pleasant start to our travels in Wyoming, but at least the bar had been set adequately low enough that I knew we could only go up from here. And up was certainly the goal, as we parked at a humble inn, not far from the towering Teton Mountain Range.

Chris met us at the inn in Dubois, planning to take us for a ride through the hills. This time, he was accompanied by one of his good friends, a man named Don who was riding an Africa Twin. I took some comfort in knowing I wasn't the person on the most inconvenient vehicle for once, and having a full sized adventure bike in the group was an assurance that we wouldn't be doing anything too insane.

Chris was kind enough to get us a room for the night so we could all leave from the same place, bright and early. I was just happy to take advantage of a hot shower and a mosquito free space. Though the sixty something bites I had gathered didn't wash off no matter how natural and exfoliating the hotel soap claimed to be.

We took a night to chat with new and old friends, then as the sun came up, we rose with it. None of us actually knew the trails or the area, despite our lofty ambitions to ride cool things, so Chris had gathered up a bunch of "Off Road Vehicle Use" maps from the local ranger station. The rangers gave him the run down, and he picked out a nice, mild 30 mile loop.

Mild is, of course, a relative term, and it wasn't long before Don and his Africa Twin were at the side of the trail discussing going off on their own. While the large adventure bikes are certainly capable of conquering wild terrain with the right rider and the right lines, they're so incredibly heavy and cumbersome, anything beyond a mildly rocky or rutted fire road often seemed to be the limits for most riders.

Which is part of why I had little qualms about using a sport bike as my primary adventure vehicle for so much of my travelling. The reality was that these "jack-of-all-trade" behemoths called "adventure" bikes rarely ventured off into anything that couldn't be done on just about any vehicle with 6+ inches of ground clearance. While the big wheels and advanced electronics made for some nice rider aids, the physical size and weight of the things didn't often inspire confidence in the kind of people who could afford to own one. And having no confidence in your ability to handle an obstacle, or in your ability to pick the bike back up if and when it inevitably falls over, makes it near impossible to let yourself really learn how to ride it.

That's part of why I had been held back in the dirt for so long, too. As I had mentioned before, my first dirt bike was a heavy pig of a CRF230. Most people would consider this an ideal beginner bike, as it's of a full size and extremely capable, but it was so tall and heavy for my physical size and strength, that I was always afraid to drop it. After the flooded carb/dead battery incident, it was a very real anxiety that was always nagging at me in the back of my mind to the point that it restricted what I was willing to try on the bike, and I never got comfortable.

It wasn't until I had tried again to learn to ride dirt on this tiny, child sized motorcycle that I found myself growing in confidence, ability, and actually starting to have fun.

There were certainly things this bike couldn't do, and there were ways that it may be holding me back from true pro-status. And I'm sure I'll have to change some of my habits once I've decided to learn to ride a taller bike. But like I've often talked about with riders who were so worried about getting a bike they will "grow into" instead of "grow out of"—It was going to be my first bike, not my last bike. Motorcycles are so easy to sell off for minimal loss after spending some time learning on them, and I'd rather hop on my dream bike with the skills and confidence to ride it well, because I developed my instincts and fear threshold on something small, than to hop on that same dream bike and always be too afraid of it to ride it properly. You slow your learning dramatically by picking a bike with your ego instead of your honest skills, and it was so elating to finally be on a bike that felt like an addition to my journey rather than a limiter.

Anyways, tangent aside, in this case, Don and his Africa Twin weren't fairing too well in the rocks, and rather than risk injury and broken bike parts, he ventured off to easier pastures, and we ventured off to much more difficult ones.

On one hand, parting ways gave us more options, but on the other, well... I'll admit that I was a little worried about what might be in store for us now that I didn't have the safety net of accommodating a full sized adventure bike.

If I were to name this ride, it would probably be something like "My Whole Life is Rocks." It was early July, and the mountains of the Shoshone National Forest were still soaked with fresh snow melt. The summer sun had arrived just enough to give the endless fields of wild flowers the warmth they needed to bloom.

We climbed long steep hills for miles, then followed wide, fast flowing roads of pea gravel. Eventually, we stopped at the top of a hill to enjoy the view and check the map.

A strange man wandered over, dressed in several coats and with what looked like many months of facial hair growth. He was walking about listlessly through the back country, and he asked for a ride into town. I wasn't sure what he was doing so far in the middle of nothing on foot, but Hollywood was the kind of guy who entertained all interactions, no matter how obviously uncomfortable they were. In this case, none of us had a back seat to spare, and we still had a lot of riding to do that day, so there wasn't much we could offer anyways.

So naturally, the man instead shifted to telling us about the grizzlies of the mountains and to be wary of riding into the trees. He finished his eerie horror stories by asking if we had any weed. I'm starting to think mountain people are as weird as us desert people. Nothing to see here. That was about the time we put back on our helmets.

Fortunately, we had packed bear spray, so I paid it little mind, and we turned off onto a wide road that swept upward into the trees.

The trail remained mostly manageable, with a few short hill climbs that had me yelling "Commit, commit, COMMIT!!!" in my helmet. I was riding faster than ever, weaving effortlessly through the imperfections in the dirt, up until we came upon our first water crossing. The deep puddle in the middle of the trail reflected the sky and the trees to perfection, which was beautiful and all, but also meant that whatever lurked below the surface was hidden by nature's painting.

But no bother. That's why I bring friends on my journeys. So they can be the guinea pigs and test the water pits.

Chris picked one line, Hollywood picked another. Both were deep and cold and bounced their tires. I shrugged and tried a third line. I may or may not have had to dab my foot in the drink to catch myself, but I made it to the other side easily enough.

Deeper into the forest, the rocks began to group up and multiply. But was it worse than North Fork?

Well...

Yeah, it actually was, but I'd been steadily improving since then, and with enough success in the rock gardens so far, I was up for the challenge. As my wheels somehow rolled over each bolder and my bike continuously righted itself, despite the monkey at the handlebars, I started to feel like my impossibly slow riding had earned me some of the balance of a trials rider. I surmounted the largest rocks I've ever had to crawl over, I kept my feet on the pegs while I did it, and I corrected my balance with my weight and inputs like in a constant dance with gravity.

It was a rare instance where I needed to touch my feet down to help leverage the bike over a rock, and when I did, it was typically only when I was scraping my skid plate. The streams became more frequent, my rooster tails became taller and faster, and my body language became increasingly more in tune with the movements of my sliding tires. I was using micro-muscles that I didn't know I had, to control the bike over terrain I didn't know I could ride on.

I bumbled through ascending and descending stone fields with a giggle in every twist of the wrist. At this point, I was so used to my rear tire being thrown around, that I not only didn't mind it, but I saw each new layout of stones as an interesting new experience in finding the balance point.

Truly, dirt biking had become my puzzle to solve.

And it was well worth the effort, too, as the mountains outside Dubois are phenomenally beautiful. Large, expansive meadows of the brightest blue lupines stretched in every direction, broken up only by the pine trees and ice cold streams. Of all the spectacular beauty I had seen on my street bike over the years, this was different. It was too far for a day hike and too rough to take the FZ. This dirt bike was likely the only way I would ever see this place.

And perhaps the challenge of it all, of balance and climbing and sliding and surviving, is what made it that much more awe-inspiring.

But nearly thirty miles into the loop, not far from the end, we came to a bit of an impasse. The first obstacle in our way even had Chris taking pause.

We parked the bikes, and took a walk to better scope it out. Beneath the permanent shade of the forest, the earth was so thoroughly soaked that every step pulled us downward into the muck. We squished and sloshed our way to a large fallen tree, two feet in diameter and standing like red tape keeping us out of the premiere.

The KTM 525 that Chris had brought this time may have been able to get over it with the right combination of luck and wheelies, but the KLX 125 wasn't even tall enough to see over the top.

But we were so close to the end! To turn around now would mean repeating the entire trail. And however confident I was becoming, the KLX has no suspension and my ass was starting to hurt. It was with determination that we continued our survey.

It didn't appear that anyone else had been through since whenever the tree had fallen. There were no ruts or tire tracks to hint at possible alternate routes. But following the flow of the trees, there were a few places where you could conceivably get around the blockage. Well, so long as you went fast enough to not sink your tire. Which is perhaps one of my greatest weaknesses, but I was feeling brave, and well, my ass really was starting to hurt.

"Let's try it." I said.

"I think we can do it." Hollywood agreed.

"If you guys are sure…" Chris shrugged.

We hiked back to the bikes and threw our legs over. There was some creativity required, some bushes to penetrate, and some big puddles to dodge, but with the right combination of solid-ish leaf cover and leveraging my bike out of swamp holes with my legs, I somehow managed to squeeze through the trees to the dry and open hillside on the other end. A round of high fives, and we continued on our way. There were just 2 more miles to go.

… And we made it about 200 more feet of them before we were staring at yet another impasse. Now, I've done my share of large rocks at this point, but these were something a bit more akin to boulders. Lopsided spheres speckled a steep slope, creating ledges that exceeded my ground clearance, and loose pebbles scattered liberally among them made sure there was minimal traction.

But there were *only* two miles to go. We had come so far. I stared at the drop off, swatting mosquitoes from the exposed skin of my neck while looking for a line I might be able to do.

"Well, I talked to the ranger about this portion yesterday…" Chris began, interrupting my thoughts. "He also suspected it might be impassable." He glanced at the trail, he glanced at his own bike, and he frowned. Then he repeated the same mantra from the last time we rode together. To press on could be fine, or it could be absolutely terrible. And sometimes stubbornness and desperation weren't good enough reasons to take huge risks that might compromise the entire day.

A valid point. And sound advice for all of life, really. Although I don't suspect I'll ever apply sound and valid advice to a majority of my life. But today, it seemed reasonable and prudent. I couldn't afford to get injured anyways, and this drop off looked like something that would very likely result in an injury.

Begrudgingly we retraced our steps, much more exhausted this time, and I lamented the seat that had transformed into what must have been the world's hardest rock as our trek stretched into its seventh hour.

Hoping to save ourselves a little pain, Chris chose a different route back. And like most shortcuts my friends seem to suggest, it ended up being far rockier and more challenging than the original way in. Every bump and buck of my bike felt like torture now, and the seemingly endless trail system was starting to feel like an insurmountable barrier instead of a bonus.

Then, finally, at the end of 55 miles over the course of nearly 9 hours that day, the longest I'd been on the little bike, we came upon a fence. Cows meandered across the trail, and a deep stream crossing cut off the edge of the ranch. My eyes fixated on the chains wrapped around the gate. Was it locked? Was this it? Did we have to turn around again?

I nearly ate shit, hitting a big rock while still rolling forward in my stunned horror. It would have been just my luck if I had conquered the hardest trail to date, then crashed on the only rock in the middle of an otherwise flat fire road.

But fortunately I caught myself and rolled to a stop, so I could better appreciate the inconvenience of my predicament. Chris stood nearby looking just as worried and stunned.

But Hollywood wasn't phased. On the contrary, he'd spent more than enough time on ranches and back roads in cow country to know to not even bat an eye at a simple gate in the woods. Instead, he crossed the stream, parked his bike at the edge, and started unwrapping the chains that, thank the heavens, were unsecured with an open pad lock.

"If they're just leasing public land, they're not allowed to lock it." He said with a pleased shrug. I exhaled long and slow. Chris did too. Then we all crossed through to the other side.

Back at the hotel, we regrouped with Don, and went to a nice dinner in town. The steak was great an all, but I wasn't there for steak.

No, that night I had earned something far greater than that. You might be thinking I'm about to give you a long diatribe on confidence or self-respect that comes from surmounting the most challenging riding you've ever done. And well, that rant can come later. Right now, all I wanted was some ice cream.

Perfect place for a picnic! The further we got into the mountains, the more spectacular it got. (Shoshone National Forest, Wyoming)

Unlike California and Colorado, where there are always tons of people around, it's easy to get lost in the hills of Wyoming (Shoshone National Forest, Wyoming)

These stream crossings were more like massive puddles—and the type that were too opaque to predict. But that oddly made them even more fun. (Shoshone National Forest, Wyoming)

When the trail no longer feels like being ridden. (Shoshone National Forest, Wyoming)

Turning around with just a few miles to go, knowing exactly how far and rough going back the way we came would be, was almost as undesirable as all the mosquitoes eating me in this photo. But much like the mosquitoes, the undesirable option won. (Shoshone National Forest, Wyoming)

Organic dirt bikes? (Shoshone National Forest, Wyoming)

If you ever want to sell someone on riding dirt, take them to mountains in the spring time. You can thank me later. (Shoshone National Forest, Wyoming)

Chapter 7

With a daring ride out of the way, we went our separate ways from Chris and Don. Being we were so close to the northern border now, we turned our nose toward Montana.

Though not without taking a cruise through Tetons National Park first. The last time I had come through this park, four years prior, the forest fires were so thick, you couldn't even see the mountains of its namesake (Which, incidentally, were named for "trois tetons" or "three nipples" by Frenchmen who thought they looked like boobs. With how jagged and pointy those mountains are, I'm not sure if the Frenchman in question had never actually seen a set of boobs, or if I should be terrified of French women).

The land was rich and green and alive with a rainbow of wild flowers that prospered in the perfect sunshine. It was a spectacular time to be in the Northwestern United States. Which was increasingly apparent by the number of tourists we were sharing the road with that day. We took a detour to the south-most entrance of the park, then we took a few hours to crawl all the way back to the top.

At times, I wished I could be riding my Yamaha in those beautiful mountains. At other times, I was glad to be able to relax in a truck, where I could both spare the attention to admire the scenery and hop out of my chair for a quick hike, without the need for a cumbersome changing ritual of armored gear and motorcycle boots.

There was sort of an interesting story to the creation of the Tetons as a National Park. Well, the park itself was uninterestingly made official back in 1929, but the meat of the story comes about twenty years later, when John D. Rockefeller Jr. bought a home in the nearby town of Jackson Hole. Now this is a town that's so prestigious these days, it's a running joke that the billionaires are chasing out all the millionaires, with some of the most elite version of gentrification in the country. But the mid-century millionaires still had a chance to own land, and Rockefeller wanted to make sure he would be one of the last to do so.

The park was originally only 96,000 Acres, encompassing the mountains themselves and little else. But when Rockefeller moved in, gazing out at these beautiful mountains before him, then conversely gazing at the homes of his neighbors with what I can only assume was scorn and a deep sigh, he determined that there was only one way to make sure his home remained beautiful.

Long story short, he bought a massive amount of the land in the valley, then after some negotiation with the understaffed and under-funded national park service, who initially didn't feel they had the resources to take care of more land, he ultimately donated another 33,000 acres to the National Park, assuring no one would ever be allowed to build homes on his view.

If that's not the definition of having "Fuck You Money," I don't know what is.

But ultimately, we all benefit from his selfishness, so I'm certainly not going to complain. In the realm of destructive things people have done with money in our country, this one is pretty saintly.

Since then, the park has expanded to 310,000 acres, as they incorporated Jackson Hole National Monument with Rockefeller's land, giving us lots to see and admire.

We toured through the park, then continued into Yellowstone, where we stopped at a handful of pretty, but violently hot and smelly, hot springs along the way. If there was still a pandemic going on, you wouldn't have known it in Yellowstone. Traffic was slow, and people were everywhere. I might have complained if the park wasn't such a visual feast of colorful bacteria, steam, and wild bison.

On the other side of this drive would be a destination we had planned since the beginning. The fourth largest state in the US (though if you ask someone who lives there, it's actually the biggest and best and most flawless no matter what the facts say) lined the northern border of the Equality State, offering both mountains and pastures. More importantly, it offered a history of glacial movement that had scraped away enough of the earth to reveal the Hells Creek Formation, where the first Tyrannosaurus Rex fossils were discovered. And if I had any say in the matter, now that we were grounded in the United States for the foreseeable future, we were going to go find the next one.

I swallowed my dread as we neared the border. As excited as I was to be a low key dinosaur hunter, I still had a lot of resentment for Montana, if I'm being honest. Well, I still do even now, if I'm being really honest. The six months I had lived in Whitefish were a low part of my life that I'll likely never forgive or get over. No matter how much I wanted to say that I had moved on after a three month trip diving in Asia to lick my wounds, the reality was that I had a near PTSD reaction to going back to this place. Memories of abandonment and depression and cruelty and xenophobia tainted all my images of Glacier and Kalispell and everything else west of the Rocky Mountains. This was a place of hate hidden behind fake smiles, religion, nationalism, and claims of old values.

But more than that, it was a place where Hollywood became a very different person, who I very much didn't like, and every time we crossed that border, I had no idea how the expectations of the people around him would change the way he treated me. The pressure to fit in had always been one of his struggles, but never was it more destructive when "fitting in" meant being permanently drunk and painfully small minded.

He used to think I was lying about the way people treated me. "You're a good person, there's no reason for them to treat you badly," he would tell me. Then without thinking, he accidentally slipped up and told someone he was from Colorado, where he had spent the majority of his life, instead of Montana where he had been born. A statement that usually gets smiles and high fives and "oh, me too!" reactions when we're travelling. Finally he got to be ostracized, ignored, and cursed at himself, and finally he had to admit that the foreign experience isn't quite the same as the local one.

Which is interesting, because as a traveller, you would never know this. The first time I ever visited Montana, I was on vacation. People treated me with kindness and warmth, because they knew I was someone who was just passing through. They loved helping people in need, and they didn't mind listening to stories of other places... so long as you didn't have some inkling to move in. The moment you shifted from a passerby to a transplant, you became a problem. They decided by default that you were going to campaign to change their laws, buy up all their property, and burn down their churches with your godless city slicker ways. It didn't matter that I was blond haired and blue eyed. It didn't matter that I was broke as hell and had no interest in politics. I was from California, so I was the devil, and by God they would chase me away.

Which, as noted, is why I left in the first place. Moving to one of the most beautiful places I had ever seen was one of the ugliest experiences I ever had, and if I could never have to relive those feelings, it would be too soon. But try as I might to explain this to Hollywood, his own sense of nationalism, having been born in North Central Montana, had him covering his ears. My trauma paired with his willful ignorance was a constant recipe for tension every time we crossed into the state.

Fortunately, he had no family in the Western side, and the big lizard fossils were all in the Eastern planes, so there was no reason we ever had to go back to that one small part of an otherwise interesting place. So as much as Hollywood insisted on visiting for the nostalgia of our miserable time there, I had grounds to refuse.

The long day in the park had us stopping into the wilderness around Big Sky for the night. Though like everywhere else, it was overflowing with campers. It was only by the grace of some strangers from North Carolina that we were able to tuck into a legal corner of the wilderness. Rangers heavily patrolled the forest to assure no one camped outside the designated areas, and we saw more than one would-be camper getting a ticket to assure there were no "parking behind a bush" shenanigans going on.

Our fellow campers also shared their fire and shelter from the sudden spurts of rain under their toy hauler awning, then we settled into our tent for a stormy night. We had hoped to ride here, but the nearby ten mile single track loop was closed to motorized vehicles for one more week. I might have thought it was close enough to opening to go for it anyway, but with the heaviness of ranger presence, I wasn't about to push our luck. We left the next morning and continued through damp, green forest land to the wide open plains, until we arrived in the small town of Augusta, just a couple hours from Great Falls.

Hollywood has a sister in Augusta, and it happened to be her fiancé's birthday, so his whole family was also in town. Having seen them barely a week prior, it wasn't much of a reunion, but it still turned into the usual frenzy. After a thorough celebration, we took a couple days with Hollywood's sister to start exploring Montana's riding scene.

Kim worked for the forest service, so she was a brilliant resource for what was available in the mountains outside Augusta. She printed out maps that... mostly made sense, and she highlighted every trail that was open to motorized vehicles. The only problem was, since no one in the park service rode motorcycles, no one knew what condition the trails were actually in. At best, they could tell us whether the trails were passable by horseback, and that was not that solid an indication as to whether they could be handled via motorbike.

With my now inflated confidence, I didn't fret too much on it though. At worst, we'd be the ones to blaze the trails if no one else had. How bad could Montana single track possibly be?

We skimmed the map, which offered a small handful of different choices. My eyes fixated on one squiggly line in particular. Norwegian Gulch, it was called. Since I couldn't ride Norway this year like I was supposed to, that would be a reasonable consolation prize. I don't know that either place had anything to do with the other, but in times like these, you cling to whatever victory you can get.

Now, Montana is not really a state of motorsports in general (yet another of the many reasons I was not able to live there), and that was astoundingly evident as we arrived at the trail head. A locked gate extended across the path, though it was easy to maneuver a bike around it through the overgrowth of weeds and wild grasses. We already had the blessing of the forest service, so I had no reason to believe we were doing anything wrong.

Though as we found ourselves flattening a barely visible single track through the field and the flowers, it became clearer and clearer that this trail likely hadn't *ever* seen a motorcycle tire in its lifetime.

Large rocks speckled a track often not even as wide as the little tire of my 125. Dodging the obstacles got more difficult as the open field began to follow the side of a hill. Roots and stones that a horse could easily step over were dangerous road blocks on the side of that mountain that left little room for deflection or error, and it was difficult to discern where the worst of it was through the overgrowth of wildflowers, bushes, and trees.

Still, the obstacles were nothing compared to Wyoming and Colorado. The road was more narrow than the single-est single track I'd encountered thus far, but I told myself that I had already done far worse terrain, and I remained committed to keep climbing. Like little braaping mountain goats, we skirted along the ledge, as the road only got more uneven and more steep. Still no problem, I thought. So long as I was focused on the road ahead, I could conquer it.

But it wasn't until I attempted to put my feet down and take a moment to re-evaluate a particularly hairy hill climb that my focus started to slip. On one side, placing my foot on the ground had my knee propped up as high as my chest. On the other side, my foot dangled freely in the weeds, with no ground to be found.

My eyes crept towards my dangling leg with slow and steady dread. I registered the stream several hundred feet below us. I registered the cliff at the end of this deceptively steep and overgrown slope. I registered the 5 inch wide trail beneath my wheels, the pokey twigs of the bush at my side, and the large roots ahead from the trees that held the hill together.

And in that moment, I registered exactly how dangerous this trail really was.

As though I had stared into the eyes of Medusa herself, my whole body began to petrify. My breathing sped up. My heart rate followed. My pupils dilated and my throat ran dry.

"We should turn around." I recall saying. Or I'm pretty sure I did. I must have, because I dropped the bike to the uphill side and crawled off of it, making it clear I was going to need some help turning around. The rewards weren't nearly impressive enough for the risk involved, and pride has no place in motorcycles, quite frankly. Fortunately, the trail widened just a touch between the trees ahead, and with Hollywood's strength and finesse, my bike was pointing home.

But we had come in a whole mile of this harrowing trail already. How I made it that far without acknowledging my predicament, I couldn't say, but while I had been confident then, now I was shaken. I remounted my bike and told myself to just paddle it out slowly. But my arms were tense on the bars, so much so that I couldn't keep the front end steady, and there was no ground to paddle on to the downhill side.

Now, one of the first rules of good motorcycle riding, be it track or street, is always to stay loose on the bars. Let the front wheel move around a bit as needed, and the physics of forward motion from the back wheel will typically correct it. As it was often described to me in road racing, you hold the bars like you would hold a baby chick. Firmly enough so it doesn't get away, but gently enough so you don't hurt it. Because if you hold on too tight, you fight the suspension and physics itself, and you can *cause* a crash by trying to stop one.

This is, of course, easier said than done when you're scared as unholy fuck. I did the chicken wing (flapping my arms while holding the bars to assure I wasn't overly tense), but my loose hold only lasted about three feet before terror had me death gripping the bars again. I couldn't seem to breathe. My eyes were starting to water. The fear had gripped me in a way that was visceral and unshakeable.

A large rock and a nervous misstep knocked my rear wheel into a bush on the downhill side of the slope, and that was enough to throw me into a panic. I managed not to cry up until I found my wheel was stuck in the branches of the shrubbery, and every attempt to free it had it digging itself slowly down the hill, threatening a point of no return. As the wheel sunk another inch downward, I let myself fall to the uphill side again and I gave in to my emotions.

I'd felt fear like this before. More than once. More than five, ten, thirty times. And I've felt it on a bike. But this was the first time I'd ever felt it on a bike in a situation that left me feeling so hopeless. I couldn't just swallow it back and press on. I was rattled so deeply that all I could see was the violent crash awaiting me through the blur of my tears. I was ready to walk back and leave my bike to the Montana wilderness.

Seeing my distress, Hollywood came up behind me and physically lifted my wheel from the brush and back onto the track. "You're okay." He reminded me. "You got here, and you can get out."

Then with a pat on the back, he added, as if reading my mind, "You can walk back and I'll relay the bikes out if I have to."

I swallowed and tried to blink the tears from my eyes. I can't begin to describe how grateful I was to have him there that day. Or for his patience and little reassurances he was giving me. He wasn't always a patient person. Actually, it was extremely rare that he was. But perhaps through this journey, he was finally starting to discover that I produce better results from being offered words of genuine encouragement and logic than from being told to man up.

With my wheel free, I swallowed hard and I continued on, but the chain reaction of panic had already been set in motion. It couldn't have been more than a few hundred feet later when that death grip was my undoing. I was white knuckling the front brake with everything I had, accidentally revving the throttle in the process, as we came upon a skinny downhill section. So when my front wheel deflected off a large rock, the jolt was just enough to knock my fingers from the brake lever and the clutch, which incidentally was the only thing holding me back from launching myself from the trail, over the edge, and straight into a nearby tree.

I was thrown from my bike, twisting my knee and testing the safety of my new armored jacket against the bark of the trees. And there I found myself, on the floor, still crying my eyes out, with my bike nearly on top of me, upside down, and thankful as hell that those trees had been there to catch me.

Thus the reason why you don't death grip your handlebars.

Hollywood helped me up. I verified all of my limbs still worked. And he made fun of me just gently enough to calm me down as I sat recovering from a miniature panic attack in the Norwegian Gulch.

He offered to ride the bikes back, but once I had taken the time to calm down and get my mind back into a comfortable state of equilibrium, I didn't have any issues riding myself out of there. It's amazing the simple things that become impossible when you're panicked.

Fortunately, my faux pas had minimal consequences, my gear doing such a great job that I didn't even end up with any new bruises. The only scars were emotional. Nothing a few years of therapy couldn't fix.

But it was quite a setback. I left Augusta not really sure where I stood in dirt biking. I had improved so much so quickly, that I had nearly forgotten I was still a total amateur. A crash course can never truly replace a lack of seat time, and a challenging and daunting side hill was certainly the kind of ride that needed a little more seat time. Or at least a little less self preservation.

Either way, I knew I had to pick myself back up by my boot buckles. Because I still had a goal to meet here in Montana, and I was sure that wouldn't be the last of the challenging, unmaintained terrain. After all, we still had to find ourselves some dinosaurs.

If you squint real hard, you can see the three nipples. But they're so pointy, they'll probably poke your eye out. (Tetons National Park, Wyoming)

Found a tree! (Augusta, Montana)

When Norwegian Gulch didn't work out, we tried following cow trails into the mountains, and that might have been even worse. (Augusta, Montana)

The one advantage to no one ever riding motorcycles in these areas was that it made for some of the most lush, untouched scenery I've ever seen. The downside, is that the trails were some of the roughest most untouched trails I've ever seen. (Augusta, Montana)

Some of the grass was so overgrown, it was catching my footpegs. (Augusta, Montana)

When cuddling in the mountains, it's always important to wear protection. (Augusta, Montana)

Chapter 8

One of my first career aspirations I ever had as a child was to be a paleontologist. It was my answer every time someone asked me what I wanted to be when I grew up, which is a pretty frequent question in US culture. Well, I told everyone I was going to be an archaeologist, since eight year old Tiff didn't know the difference, but I think most second graders dreamed of hunting down dinosaur bones after they made it through the unit in school about ancient lizards. The ten thousand "Land Before Time" movies I watched on repeat, paired with the dragons in video games and frequent trips to the nearby La Brea Tar Pits (a dinosaur museum in Los Angeles, where there's an active tar pit still being excavated for fossils), only added to that obsession.

I had no idea what being a paleontologist actually entailed beyond the fantastical depiction in Jurassic Park, but I was certain it was all I wanted to be. It wasn't until I was in my teens that my career focus shifted to wanting to do concept art for video games. And then it wasn't until my late teens and early twenties that the reality of the world and having to make a survivable income shifted my focus to Software Development.

I liked working in Tech. As I've noted in the past, I was a hardcore gamer my whole life, and living through virtual means was how I defined myself. But it wasn't until I committed my entire existence to riding motorcycles that I discovered, ironically, that a career in exploration and studying the stories and creatures of history would make far more sense for my personal happiness. Ironically, I did make my life into an adventure when I grew up. And now I was going to make it into an adventure that involved searching for dinosaur bones.

It's funny how sometimes our youngest selves understand the needs of our soul better than our adult selves ever will.

That said, when we were sitting in quarantine and I was busy internally sobbing and licking my wounds, as I desperately wished the world would reopen and I could go off on the road trip of all my hard work and dreams, Hollywood proposed this whole dirt bike trip as an alternative. And the only way I was able to convince myself that I was okay with it was if it resulted in finding a real dinosaur bone out in the wild. I'd heard the local legends and wives tales of skulls and leg bones being found in the Montana rivers and wilds. And now I wanted to see it for myself.

But truth be told, I had no idea what to actually look for. While there was always the once in a lifetime possibility we might just stumble on a large obvious bone on our Sunday stroll, I wanted to know what the real dinosaur hunters looked for. And how better to do that than to take a trip down Montana's "Dinosaur Trail," a route through the state that hits fourteen different dinosaur themed museums. The first in the circuit was in the town of Choteau (Pronounced Show-Tow if you don't want to be shunned as an outsider), and the second was just north of there in the much smaller town of Bynum.

The Two Medicine Dinosaur Center was a small building that wasn't terribly noteworthy beyond the dinosaur statue that sat outside. We walked through the doors to a small wrap around desk, and we paid the $7 donation fee to take a tour. There were only two rooms. One housed fossils from mammals and small dinosaurs behind glass cases. The other held the Two Medicine claim to fame. The Seismosaurus was one of the largest and longest dinosaurs ever discovered, after being unearthed in New Mexico in 1979. But the Two Medicine Dinosaur center happened to house the skeletal model, which was so massive, its vertebrae weaved and stretched through the entire building. There were a handful of other bones on display that had been found locally, including some nests from the nearby "egg mountain" where an entire family of Hadrosaurus skeletons were found, after all of them had theoretically been wiped out in a swift catastrophic event. And then there was the lab, which you could see from behind a window, where various specimens were displayed in plaster cast casings in different phases of excavation and restoration.

Once we had our fill, we returned to the office where we could sign up to join the museum for a dig. In motorcycle racing, we often sign up to take classes with professionals to learn and improve on our craft, and I saw no reason that fossil hunting would require any less dedication. How better to learn how to identify dinosaur bones than to go out with a group of paleontologists? It wasn't the cheapest tour, but in my mind, it was a way of making a commitment.

We showed up the next morning with some sun block and an appetite for adventure. We loaded into a van with some other tourists, and they drove us out into the prairies.

Our first stop was a wide, slopping field, publically owned by the state. Because this was public land, none of the bones found there could be removed without having to send them to another museum that had "repository status." Basically, Two Medicine had not yet gotten government approval to store or keep bones for an extended period of time, so any bones they brought back would be shipped off to a larger museum in the state (In the case of Montana, that would be the museum in Bozeman). As a result, all of the bones in this area had been left undisturbed for whenever they might manage to get that status, where they would then perform a much more thorough excavation of the specimens.

On one hand, from a financial and pride based perspective, I could fully understand why it was worth it to them to wait on a physically intensive excavation until they were allowed to keep the fruits of their labor. But on the other hand, from a scientific perspective, I couldn't understand how they justified the very real risk of letting the now exposed bones break down and get destroyed by the harsh weather patterns of Montana. It was one thing to have found a place where bones are still buried and thus protected from the elements. It was another to leave them sitting in open air.

But I suppose it comes down to what's more important—is it about preserving history in the name of science? Or is it about getting the fame and glory for doing it?

Not even scientists are immune to the draw of grandeur. If anything, many people likely got into science based fields with the hopes of accomplishing something grand. So I can't fault them for wanting to get the glory. It was just unfortunate that government laws intending to help save our history from being destroyed in the name of money and selfish hoarding has instead let our history crumble under the weight of its paperwork.

Anyways, this field was rife with fossils, and it wasn't a long walk before we stopped upon our first spattering of bones. These chunks on the hillside were what are known as "Float Fossils." Basically, that means that most the dinosaur's remains are somewhere uphill of these fossils, but the erosion of the earth over time has allowed the first few pieces to "float" to the surface. As a writer, I'll resist calling out the obvious misuse of what the word "float" actually means and just point out how nice it is that landslides are doing all the work. So for future reference, when you find bones resting in open air, down slope with no digging required, you can generally assume that if you follow the hill side nearby, that's where the rest of the bones will be.

The lead paleontologist picked up a bone and passed it around. When it came to me, I stood in awe as I felt a real, legitimate dinosaur bone in the palm of my hand. It was a piece of a femur, they presumed. The surface was smooth, but you could still distinguish the cellular structure of the bones. Organic parallel lines streaked along the length of it, and a porous, hardened-yet-sponge-like marrow rested inside.

The bone had been colored with a copper like color by the replacement of minerals over the years. Bones preserved in different mineral make ups would take on different colors to reflect that, some more white, some more reddish, some even black.

For all intents and purposes, if I had seen such a specimen while walking through this field on any other day, I would have thought it was simply a rock. It resembled sandstone more than any obvious animal. But the more closely we examined it, the more obvious it became that these were skeletal remains.

It wasn't long before we were identifying the rocks on the hill side as bones all by ourselves. We searched the tall, unkempt grass for traces of long gone creatures, and came up with ribs, with arms, and with teeth. Anything that was questionable, we could use the lick test—that is to say, licking my finger, then touching it to the bones to see if my finger would stick. Bones are porous, so the saliva created a light suction as it seeped into the bones pores when touching a wet finger to the bones.

I wasn't literally licking the bones to see if they tasted dinosaur-ish or anything, I swear.

We finished the day with dental picks and paint brushes, in a scene that could have been ripped from the opening of Jurassic Park. The museum was actively excavating a dinosaur nest they had found on a nearby rancher's property, and they were hoping it might be so lucky as to have intact eggs. It was a particularly delicate find, so while my instincts wanted to dig like a dog on a mission to uncover their favorite bone, we sat there under the hot sun for hours, chipping away at small bits of loose dirt, and shoveling the disappointing mounds into a bucket for removal.

Unable to sit still that long, Hollywood wandered off on the hillsides, looking for more dramatic finds. It wasn't long before he was shouting back to the camp with pieces of a rib cage. It was bizarre to me how incredibly easy it really was to find the bones. They were everywhere, staring you right in the face, if you had the faintest idea of where to look.

We rode back to the museum, gushing about the day, and feeling incredibly confident that we could replicate this out in the wild. I didn't know how hard it might be to pinpoint spots to start searching, but we took note of the geological maps detailing Montana's land formations and hoped we could figure it out.

As we drove away that day, heading for our next destination, I sat and reflected. It's incredible to hold a seventy-something million year old bone in your hand and imagine what the world was once like. And what catastrophic but lucky combination of events made it possible to connect that world with mine. So often I'm in awe of the world we live in when I travel. Not simply the beauty it's created, but the violence it's endured. From fire and brimstone to frozen tundras to the beautiful paradise we call home today, our planet is a true testament to what you can become if you keep on fighting.

The stories the land could tell. I wish I could know them all.

The museum was small, but they had some impressive skeletons on display. (Bynum, Montana)

And here we see a rare moment where Hollywood is perfectly still. (Bynum, Montana)

They called this the puzzle bone, as they found it in four cleanly broken pieces. (Bynum, Montana)

This gigantic femur bone was once used as a fencepost by a farmer in Wyoming, before they realized it wasn't just a conveniently shaped rock. (Bynum, Montana)

The Two Medicine Formation didn't look like much from the surface, but this field was full of fossils, sink holes, and crumbling badlands. (Bynum, Montana)

Bones are somewhat easy to identify by their still preserved cellular structure. (Bynum, Montana)

This is a vertebrae, which had "floated" out of the nearby hill side. (Bynum, Montana)

Getting to join the paleontologists on a dig for a newly discovered dinosaur nest was the field trip of 8-year-old Tiff's dreams. (Bynum, Montana)

Chapter 9

From Bynum it was a straight shot along Highway 2 to the town of Havre. We stopped into Shelby along the way for dinner at one of the oldest Chinese restaurant in the United States, an unexpected highlight in a land of steak and bar food (the number one oldest in the US is actually in Butte, Montana. It might be surprising to learn a place as homogenous as Montana has the oldest Chinese restaurant in the country, but if you consider the number of Chinese immigrants who worked to build the railroad through the western United States, it makes more sense), then we cruised across the long stretch of rolling wheat fields to the windy city on the high line.

This railroad town, just a stone's throw from the Canadian border, was Hollywood's hometown. There was little there of note outside the train station and the underground city that had been built to escape fires that ran rampant in the area 100 years ago.

But what it *did* offer was the Judith River Formation, a geological formation that was known to be rich with prehistoric fossils. A majority of the creatures here were more aquatic than what we found in the Two Medicine Formation, with prehistoric snails and alligators and other large and small finned creatures. Here, the crumbling badlands revealed bones naturally as the winds and winters eroded away the earth, creating endless possibilities for finding these long lost creatures.

So naturally, we decided to go to the nearby Fresno OHV Park, just a few miles outside of town, to try our hand at finding some on our own. Worst case, we wouldn't find anything, but would still get to do hooligan things on our dirt bikes. So it was a solid win win.

Fresno OHV is a "top down" kind of park, where you park atop a plateau in the middle of the badlands, then ride down the abrupt slopes into the valleys below on the loose, black, vegetation devoid soil. The park appeared to be all but completely abandoned, being it was a gorgeous Saturday in the early summer, and yet we were the only people to show up there the entire day. Montana is not exactly a culture of exploration or recreation, so this wasn't surprising. But when coming from a place like Colorado or California, where people are doing their best to get outside and climb every mountain, ride every trail, and swim in every lake, it's always a bit surprising to be in a fascinating and unique new riding area where no one bothers to ride. On one hand, it's a peaceful and wonderful escape. On the other hand, it's a bit sad to see a lack of curiosity and wonder for the outside world.

Though while the complete disinterest in motorsports (or anything that wasn't alcohol, football, and 'Merica related, really) was a huge part of why I hated living in this state, incidentally, it was also the reason we were able to come here hunting bones. No one was out adventuring and searching for dinosaur fossils, even though their own backyard was full of them, so someone like me could show up with my abject curiosity in this advanced age of the year 2020, and I could still happen upon lost and ancient treasures, sitting in plain sight in the wild. The lack of people also meant I had plenty of time to *look* for treasures without being disturbed, and more significantly, it gave me plenty of time to try to confront my next fear: The long, loose, and steep downhills.

I'd been doing a lot of rocky down hills lately, but rarely were they this long, never were they this steep, and they certainly weren't this unpredictable. The dirt compacted and crumbled like riding through popcorn, and it was a battle of my mental demons every time I inched toward the edge and stared down vertical drops. Every moment I looked at the slope, my resolve to roll down it weakened. There was nothing at the bottom of particular concern, so even if I got out of sorts, it's not like I was going to crash into anything, but surrendering my wheels to the whims of gravity takes quite a bit more trust than my rough childhood traumas had instilled in me.

But there was a prize to be won, and this purely mental barrier would not be what stopped me. With a few breaths longer than a five count (okay, more like a ten count), I pushed off the edge and let my bike roll. I focused on the rear brake to try to modulate my speed, but my bike was gaining momentum regardless of my commands. After a point, even fully locking the rear didn't matter anymore, as the loose crumbling mud offered no traction to grab on to. The bike barreled downward at speeds that felt out of control, even though they were probably something akin to 20mph, and every descent felt like an exercise in near death. I lamented the hill climbs that would require new drop ins, and my mind was a cloud of stress. The only thing I had going for me here was that my desire to live out my dreams to be a treasure hunter far outweighed even my most acute panic signals. Plus, after that traumatizing last ride at Norwegian Gulch, I was perhaps a bit hell bent on redeeming myself.

But this was more like a redemption for clowns. First order of business, I got my bike stuck in a bog and had to dismount and walk it out. My second order of business involved a deep, opaque mud puddle and an unpredictably tall step up. The puddle was deep and the step up was taller than the 125's front wheel, so no one will be surprised when I say I hit that climb like a bird slamming into a tree. My bike reared back like an angry horse and landed on its side, propped up vertically by the mud hill. I was promptly discarded *in* the mud puddle, with the bike partially jammed against my leg.

I thanked the god of speed for dirt bike armor this day.

Hollywood helped me wrench the bike upward and onto the other side of the pit, and I climbed out with my head hung low. The fact that I had crashed was whatever. The fact that this meant I did not earn ice cream this day was much more devastating.

Can't win 'em all, I suppose.

But once I was on the other side of the badlands roller coaster, the park opened up into an expansive valley. We cruised along to the bank of the Milk River, until any semblance of a trail had all but completely disappeared. By the slow flowing water, we enjoyed a picnic of water and granola, then we circled back to start combing the badlands for fossils.

A cow femur, a coyote skull, some glistening, rainbow sea shell fossils, and a heart shaped rock or two were fine rewards in and of themselves, but they weren't what we were looking for. We crossed the valley and continued the search, occasionally stopping to more thoroughly survey the eroded valley walls.

Nothing. Nothing. Nothing.

Maybe this was going to be a lot more difficult than I imagined.

We started heading back, splitting up on occasion to cover more ground. It wasn't until we had nearly retraced our steps all the way back to the parking lot when Hollywood rode up behind me honking his horn.

Of course, he did this exactly as I had just cleared one of the most difficult hill climbs of the ride. I contemplated for a moment if I was more intrigued by the concept of finding bones or of not having to surmount that hill again. It was a tight competition. But ultimately, I chose the bones.

I barreled back down the hill, keeping my tires steady to avoid a large ditch that split the descent, then I followed him to a nondescript slope in the badlands.

And there, among a couple dried shrubs on a mound of dark grey popcorn dirt, was a fragment of a bone.

As we searched more we found not just one piece but two. Then three. Then eight.

We found something! We really had!

But could there be more?

My eyes scanned every rock and peddle that looked suspicious, parsing the smooth, cellular bone structure from chunks of sand stone. Instead of chasing the source, I followed the float fossil trail downward to the hard, dry ground at my feet.

A glistening black in the sun bleached earth caught my eye. It was small enough to seem inconsequential, but interesting enough to merit further investigation. With a careful finger and a little digging help from one of those heart shaped rocks, I freed the smooth, shiny object from the hardened soil.

Blade like serrations lined one side of the fossilized enamel, following the elegant curvature of a predator tooth.

I want to say I screamed at this point. Maybe jumped up and down.

But I think I actually just stared at it wide eyed in too much shock and excitement to actually manifest either of those gestures. But what's important here is that I had found a tooth! A real live dinosaur tooth!

The size and shape was small enough that it was unlikely to be from any sort of Tyrannosaurus Rex or anything as cool as that. But given the amphibious, underwater nature of the Judith River Formation, it could very well have been some sort of prehistoric alligator fang. Or maybe Montana had a loch ness monster or miniature Godzillas.

We took a picture to remember it by, then I pressed the fossil back into the dirt, in hopes of preserving it until it could be excavated further. Then Hollywood and I high fived, before we strapped back on our helmets and headed back to the car.

I turned off my gopro and stared again at the picture of that tooth with complete and utter disbelief.

Day one and dino hunting was already a success! I never thought this was such an attainable dream!

Being amateur professional paleontologists is way more fun when you get to do it on a dirt bike. (Havre, Montana)

Badlands are prime dinosaur hunting territory, but not so prime traction having territory. (Havre, Montana)

Eventually the vague barely discernable tracks turned into rocks and riverside quicksand, and that's about where we called it good. (Havre, Montana)

The Milk River weaves through such a large portion of the Judith River Formation, I can only imagine the fossils that have been both uncovered and swept away naturally over the years. (Havre, Montana)

I can't be sure, but I think my dirt bike might have Fainting Goat Syndrome. (Havre, Montana)

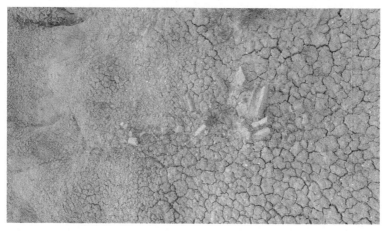

This is a perfect example of float fossils as they appear, undisturbed, in the wild. I'll just say I might have screamed a little. Or maybe a lot. Impossible to say. (Havre, Montana)

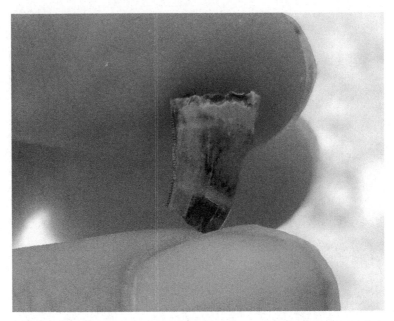

*A tooth! You can even see the small serrations on one side!
Finding one of these in the wild is like finding a specific
strand of hay in a hay stack. Based on what we saw in
museums, my guess is a prehistoric Alligator Tooth.
(Havre, Montana)*

Chapter 10

Now, imagine you're a pirate who just discovered a buried treasure, just outside the gates of El Dorado. Would you stop yourself at just one measly little doubloon? Or would you latch onto that shit like a pit bull and double down, concocting an elaborate heist plan to take the whole city?

In Havre, we were just a few miles from Fort Peck, and Fort Peck housed what's known as the "Hells Creek Formation." This was the formation where all of the legendary creatures of every second grader's most vivid fantasies were found. The Tyrannosaurus Rex, the Triceratops, the Stegosaurus—the giants of our planet's past all rested here, nestled into a beautiful grave around a beautiful lake.

And after physically holding the tooth of a creature millions of years past in my hand, getting that rush of success and possibilities pumping through my veins, I couldn't help at least taking a peek in the treasure trove.

Though the treasure was not without its guardians. While the development of farm land had long since run off the once prominent Grizzly Bear population, what stood in its place were millions and millions and millions of grasshoppers, mosquitoes, and deer flies. I once thought a night of swatting away mosquitoes was one of nature's greatest tortures, but let me tell you, the deer flies are worse. So much worse. They were not only aggressive, but those bites stung like a thousand bee stings. And you didn't get to suffer just one or the other either. The mosquitoes and the deer flies had no trouble existing in chaotic harmony, so you had the unique opportunity to itch while you cried.

But you don't find dinosaur bones on the floor of the Holiday Inn (And I couldn't afford one even if you could), so we still stuck around to camp out. We built our portable home by the water's edge, and we sifted through sand and shoreline for any fossils that may have been naturally revealed by erosion. We found fragments of sea creatures here and there—the sparkling shells of squid and mollusks were abundant—but mostly we just found that deer fly bites are excruciating.

Fort Peck reservoir is quite large, and shaped with hundreds of jagged inlets and tendrils. So to circle that lake, following the shoreline to any degree, took several days of driving in and out and in and out of often extremely unmaintained roads. We clocked in at over a thousand miles of roads that were so ravaged and washed out, even our KLXs would have had a rough time.

We tried using the paper maps from the local museums to find our way around, but even though these maps had been last updated only a year or two prior, it only took one harsh Montana winter to have rendered half the roads impassable, non-existent, and dramatically overgrown. We'd follow the squiggly white lines into an inlet, and I'd find myself in a cold sweat while staring at the storm clouds overhead, the cliff at our side, the mud on our tires, and Hollywood tapping the four wheel drive button. In other spots, the road was washed out completely, as old broken culverts made no attempt to protect the narrow land bridges from water logging.

We spent more time searching for passable roads than we did for dinosaur bones, occasionally backtracking hours of time to go only a few miles of distance. As much enthusiasm as I had in the beginning, hundred degree days, the bugs, and the fruitless hunts in the surrounding badlands started to squash my motivation.

If it hadn't been so hot, and if every road didn't require hundreds of miles between fuel stations, we might have taken our dirt bikes to make this a bit more fun than it was daunting. But the nature of being in the middle of nothing for large distances meant we were better off in the comfort of our 4-wheel-drive Chevy.

I'd complain that this went against the heart of the trip, but I appreciated the bug protection that the doors and windows provided.

Rather than be a scavenger hunt and a training montage, Fort Peck was more of a return to our roots, where we'd camp beneath the scorching sun, then cool off by skinny dipping in the ice cold lake.

Fort Peck Reservoir itself was a beautiful place, no matter what angle or direction you came at it from. Every local had a story, real or likely imagined, of a time they stumbled upon massive intact dinosaur skeletons while simply lazing about on the river banks, and the sheer size of the place meant we finally got to camp in solitude and silence. The pandemic had triggered such a mad rush on outdoor activities, that it had been a long time since we had been able to sit around our own camp fire in peace, and simply enjoy each other's good company. No matter how many hours, days, months, and years that we spent together, I never got tired of our time alone, just he and I, in beautiful tranquility.

Whether we were chatting away, sitting together in silence, or dancing to the same ten songs, part of what made these big adventures so enjoyable was being able to share them together. Our relationship had had ups and downs—In Montana specifically, those downs had nearly been enough to throw the whole thing away—and a majority of those struggles came about when we had to spend too much time apart.

Some people prefer a lot of space in a relationship. They're content to live completely separate lives, going on extravagant vacations or trips without the other person, and simply having a consistent person to come home to. But for me, I guess even in this regard, I was a woman of great extremes. I could be a bit all or nothing. Or at least, I wanted to share all parts of my life with someone when I could—spend as much time together as physically possible, bond over a majority of our hobbies, and never have to exclude the other person. Be it motorcycles or scuba diving or any big adventure from here, I wanted someone who would be my ride or die bitch. And if I couldn't have that, I'd rather just be single and alone completely.

I enjoyed our time in the lakeside wilderness, but by the time we had finished circling the lake, we still had little to show for it. We brought some of our more questionable "Are these bones?" type finds into a museum in Malta, where the head paleontologist took some educated guesses on what we may have found. But all we came up with were shards of sparkling amber, some petrified wood, and some pre-historic sea shells.

We tried to make the trip a smidge more worthwhile by fooling around at a very small OHV park outside Glasgow, the next town over. The park only spanned about 40 acres of space, much of which was spent in elevation, so it was more of a place to simply stave off rust, opposed to being one of those all day adventures. Hollywood took a bit of a digger, barreling down a fresh track on the hillside straight into a ditch (probably why the track was fresh, eh?), but aside from that, it wasn't a terribly noteworthy place. Great if you were a local kid who wanted somewhere to practice your hill climbs after school, but not worth much more than an hour of time if you're a traveller looking for unique and exciting places to explore.

There were no bones here, though. Just grass and hills and rocks and more mosquitoes. We opted to get a room for the night at a shoddy small town motel to shower and recover from our time with the mosquitoes and deer flies and summer storms. It was the kind of place that still had a bulky CRT TV on its dated night stand, springs that poked through the surface of its ancient mattress, and a shower with all the water pressure of a pissing dog, but when you've lived in a truck and a tent long enough, even that feels like luxury.

At this point, we'd found lots of fragments of bones in Montana, but like any over-ambitious person, now I wanted more. A tooth or a piece of an unidentified chunk-a-saurus was exciting, but it wasn't the kind of find that made my jaw drop anymore. I wanted to see a bone that I could piece together. Something intact. Something identifiable. Something that felt like a real, honest to god *animal*.

But what are the chances that we, some two-bit hacks and haphazard adventurers, would be able to find something that trained and attentive paleontologists hadn't? These small bits were easy, but they were so damaged and uncertain that the local museums didn't even give pause when brought to their attention. The rule said that anything less than three bones wasn't worth the time or resources, and I wanted to find something that *was* worth their time and resources.

It's not like I expected fame or glory. I just had a bad habit of constantly upping the ante when I liked something. Motorcycles are fun—let's go to the race track! Cross Country trip? Let's go around the whole world! Swimming is fun—let's learn to scuba dive! Hiking is peaceful—let's fly to a foreign country and climb Mount Fuji! I like writing—well fuck, look where we are now.

You get the picture. So just imagine the way finding a few little pieces spiraled into obsession.

Though having already searched the OHV park and only found small and scattered remains, I had no clue where that mother load might be hiding.

We took another drive down to the badlands by Winifred, where we took our truck across a ferry and ran into some cowboys searching for their lost cows, but aside from some mild comedy, those badlands didn't produce anything any more interesting than what we'd already come across.

With no other ideas in mind, we returned to Havre to figure out what we wanted to do next. We could check off finding a dinosaur from my bucket list, technically, regardless of my unreasonable, snowballing expectations, so perhaps it was about time we simply moved on. Besides, the limited selection of fried bar food that comprised every menu in every restaurant in what felt like the entire state wasn't doing my health or my energy any favors, and I was starting to think I was going to get scurvy if we didn't make our way back to somewhere with fruits and vegetables.

We set up camp at Fresno Lake, just outside Havre, and we settled in beneath the full moon. These were my favorite conditions for contemplating where we were going in life.

Ultimately, we decided we may as well at least get in one more ride before we left. Hollywood had a good friend who lived in Havre, and he and his young son just so happened to ride dirt bikes.

Jeff and his boy showed up at the lake bright and early one fine Saturday, and they unloaded a couple of bikes by our camp spot. This wasn't specifically an off road park, but there was a single trail that jutted up into the surrounding badlands that went some indeterminate distance. I would have been content to just ride along the rocky beach, but something about a trail gives you a bit more sense of purpose than aimless fooling around. Free riding is enjoyable, but trails offer a set goal, so there was more of a sense of purpose and achievement when you were done.

Once we climbed the first hill, it wasn't long before we found ourselves in the thick of nothing. Dead and dried plants lined a road made of sand about as wide as a pickup truck, with sporadic rocks place generously on top the trail. As you might expect, the road narrowed as the terrain worsened. It wasn't long until we found ourselves traversing an extended roller coaster of constant ups and downs, with only the briefest reliefs throughout.

Hollywood, who had started the morning a few cocktails deep, as culture seemed to dictate in Montana, took off without any mind for the rest of us. Jeff stayed back with his son, helping him with encouragement and morale boosts on each daunting drop. I was a smidge faster than them, but a smattering slower than Hollywood, so not long into the ride, I found myself in the middle of a series of steep sandy descents and steeper sandier ascents, totally alone.

Every time I attempted to commit to the drop, my wheels bucked and squirmed at alarming speeds, leaving me to feel completely out of control no matter how many times I succeeded.

To add to this, there's a different feeling when you're out in the wilderness alone. When there's no one in shouting distance to help you, and the conditions have you already feeling like you're in over your head. If I wasn't highly prone to anxiety, this may have been my moment to step up to the bat and prove to myself that I could do it.

Maybe I'd get off on being alone against the world and every obstacle conquered, no matter how poorly, would feel like another ring in my chainmail. I often felt this way when I was riding on the road, in an environment where I'm confident and brave and comfortable and looking for the next challenge.

But in the dirt, where I was about as comfortable as a man who had his head in a guillotine, this very small moment of intense solitude, while barreling out of control down a steep sandy hill, was my personal hell. I couldn't have made it more than a mile in before I was parking my bike to try to calm myself down and collect myself.

Even the hill climb portions, where gravity worked with me to keep me at a slow and not scary pace, which were usually my mental forte, felt more daunting than enjoyable. The length and grade had me often paddling the bike to propel it the last few feet as the engine ran out of steam several feet from the crest. Knowing this trail didn't loop and that I would have to go back down these same climbs only added to that feeling of dread. My brain was piling up a laundry list of things to be scared of in the near future, while still wrestling with the things I was scared of now.

Perhaps if there had been something interesting and eye catching about this trail beyond the uphill, downhill, uphill, downhill, it might have been more enjoyable. I could have justified the pain with pretty lies like "I never could have experienced such wonder without this threatening, spiteful machine!" But... there really wasn't. Vegetation was dead, the views were dead, there were no dinosaur bones, and it was boiling hot out.

Hollywood had taken off ahead with the backpack that held all the water, so I sat down by my bike in protest, battling heat exhaustion and grasshoppers that tried to nest in my hair. My morale dwindled to a point of critical displeasure. It was going to take a lot of chocolate and cheerleading to reverse this.

Eventually, Jeff and his son caught up. A few moments more than "eventually" Hollywood at long last circled back to check on us.

Jeff's son had been having similar problems with the hills. He had the easy confidence that most children have—you know, the kind that you have before you've gathered a heap of knee injuries and know the cost of medical bills—but he had none of the know how to get up or down them. He would freeze up for a few moments at the tipping point, then with a death grip on the bars, he would do his best to inch down as slowly as he could.

Ordinarily I took comfort in having others who shared my struggles, but eight-year-old boys who won't admit they're as scared as their body language clearly communicates is not as helpful as, say, a fellow adult who no longer has useless things like pride.

So I got back on my bike, surrounded by the "it's fine, bro!" crowd, and begrudgingly tried to continue.

But there comes a point in anxiety where you get sick of being told how easy something is. When you're struggling with panic attacks and mental demons and reach a point of near (or more than near) tears, and someone comes up to you to tell you this is a total breeze, it's not helpful. It doesn't fire you up. It compounds your anxiety. It makes you angry at yourself and your brain that can't process all these things as "easy" and "fine" like they can. It makes you resentful towards the person who diminishes the fact that you're struggling and mocks you when you can't do something they find oh so simple.

Did that person really do something wrong? No.

They didn't support you in a way that you needed them to, sure, but their only real crime is not struggling the way you struggle. Or lacking the empathy to understand that. But when you're trying to learn and you're the only person who sucks, it's disheartening to the point that I found myself just wanting to give up. I had no desire to press on or better myself that day. I wanted to quit and shove the bike back in the truck and go home to my FZ-07.

It had been so refreshing to ride with Carolanne all those weeks ago, where we were able to figure out how to conquer obstacles together. It was refreshing to have someone admit that they struggle too, so I didn't have to feel completely alone and like a burden to the group. This wasn't fun anymore. It was "Tiff's fear and riding skills are ruining the day, even for innocent children," and it just sucked.

This is possibly one of the worst side effects of the anxious mind. Not only does it sometimes paralyze me with fear to the point that I can't perform in a way that I want to, but it gives me an extra intense sense of social anxiety when I'm surrounded by people who I now feel are being let down by me. It's a compounding equation of frustration and a cycle of self-loathing that helps no one.

I forced myself to press on, wearing a fake smile and continuing down into another valley. We shimmied along a decaying cliff side, and I found myself walking the bike at half a mile an hour in an effort to not overshoot the turn. On the other side was a ledge that overlooked another part of the lake. The trail dead ended there. The lake was too far down the cliff to take a dip to cool off, while the trail had degraded to just wild grass and rocks.

With nowhere to go but home, we turned around. The hills that felt like climbing a wall on the way in were now everything I could do to keep it together as I went down them. It was on a prayer that I made it back to the truck at all, and I was glad to be off the bike when I did. All the desire I had to ride around the beach was gone. I never thought I would say this, but... I miss rocks. The refreshing stream crossings and the tall tree roots, and the sticky mud were interesting obstacles. They were puzzles that focused on balance and analysis in order to pass each test.

But these steep hills were more about adrenaline and thrills and speed than they were about careful methodology. Try as I might to get used to it, even after surviving multiple drops, I hated this kind of riding. I was scared of this kind of riding.

I thought I had gotten past these kinds of demons. I thought dirt bikes were going to be fun now. But turns out, there's still a lot of terrain I'm not at all comfortable on, and with the right cocktail of steep, hot, and ugly, I'm still ready to opt out of this hobby.

Jeff said his goodbyes and drove home, while I stared listlessly at the lake before me. There was more to discover in Montana, sure, but not in the form of Tiff-friendly riding.

For a state that was comprised almost entirely of flat wheat fields, that got the name "Big Sky" due to the open landscape that was unencumbered by hills or trees, Montana's off roading had oddly been the steepest and most daunting riding to date. The wild, untamed, and unpopulated quality of their trails and OHV areas meant that every ride was like paving a new path in the wide open plains, and the nature of badlands meant that those wide open plains often dropped off into perilous no man's lands. I just wasn't skilled enough yet for Montana. I had a lot of learning to do.

To pass the rest of the day doing something I enjoyed, we instead shifted to searching the shoreline for dinosaur bones again. The occasional fragment was speckled about here and there. A smooth brown, broken rib bone, a fragmented humerus, a chunk of vertebrae down below the rocks. Cool finds, sure, but nothing that would get the local paleontologists to take notice.

We made our way along the perimeter, then started scouring a large rock pile atop an island that had been exposed by the low water levels of early August.

The large, sheet-like rocks weren't likely to budge, but under the smaller rocks, we could easily skim the ground for fossils.

"Hey! Check this out!" Hollywood called to me from a few feet away. I tossed a bit of not-quite-bone sandstone back into the wet sand, then walked over.

The smallest bit of red protruded from the ground between scattered stones. It was smooth. The streaks of cellular structure flowed purposefully along the surface.

It was unmistakable. This was a bone. But how much of one?

I took off my backpack and kneeled on the ground, both of us fixated on this potential find. Hollywood lifted a rock out of the way. I used my fingers to brush away some excess sand. Below the surface there was more. It wasn't simply a small chunk that washed up on shore.

We pulled some old tooth brushes from my backpack, and I went to work. I dragged some sand away with my fingers, then used the brush to dust off the rest. The length of the bone kept growing, every scoop or brush of sand revealing a little more. I followed the contours of the bone, as it splintered off into more shapes. More bones. And bigger ones.

Hollywood wandered off to get our chairs, but I was too fixated to stop now. I dug like I had just found a

144

pirate's treasure that could set me up for my entire life. My brush traced the gentle bend of a rib that extended beyond what I assumed was some sort of angular leg. Another route of bones poked out from the top end. I slipped a finger along the diameter, feeling for a bottom in the heavy wet sand that held it. It was thicker than my hand could wrap around, and about as long as my entire leg.

There was one bone. Two. Then three.

THREE!

I sat back and stared at our prize. No more digging was necessary. I had the evidence I needed to get professional eyes on this now.

A child ran by with his parents. A teenager climbed on the rocks to take an Instagram photo. No one noticed the massive bones before me. No one asked. No one cared. I was staring at an unmistakable dinosaur bone in the middle of a popular boat launch at a popular lake on a Saturday, and not a soul noticed the piece of long lost history standing prominently in the land.

Yep, still not a culture of explorers. But it was no matter. If no one else wanted any of that exciting glory spattered around, I suppose I could take on the burden of victory for them.

This was the big one. This is why we came here.

Once I had uncovered just enough to make it clear that this was a find worth paying attention to, I took pictures from different angles and noted the exact coordinates in hopes that we might excite some of the local authorities. I knew there was no way to extract this bone ourselves in a way that was safe and non-destructive. Even if there had been, that was illegal, and I'm still a surprisingly lame, authority respecting, goody two shoes, considering I'm a biker.

Plus, I was too excited to risk a mistake, and I wanted to make sure this creature we found got excavated properly. The same curiosity that kept digging and digging, laid flat in the dirt in my bikini, not even caring how much sand was getting in my suit, was the curiosity that wanted to know what this bone belonged to. It could have been a simple hadrosaurus, sure. But it also could have been something entirely new. This little island in the lake could be an entire nest of dead dinosaurs, for all I knew, and we could be sitting on a discovery of a lifetime.

Whatever the case, I wanted to know.

I gently reburied the bone to keep it safe from the elements, while Hollywood hiked up the hill to the nearest blip of phone service, where he dialed the paleontologist we had talked to at the museum in Malta, in hopes of getting someone who could legally extract the skeleton to come take a look at it. But like all things that involve the government, we were sent on a wild goose chase of inefficient red tape. The paleontologist directed us to the Bureau of Land Management. The Bureau of Land Management directed us to the Bureau of Reclamation.

Unfortunately, in the coming weeks, the initial excitement was quickly buried under government bureaucracy. The local paleontologist had practically been jumping for joy when he saw the photos, but Bozeman's repository claimed it had no room for new specimens, and the Bureau of Reclamation claimed to have no time or resources to allot to it. Montana's digging season was exceptionally short, as they were prone to six months or more of snow and subfreezing temperatures every year, and they were exceptionally understaffed, being a state with more cows than humans. I would have been happy to volunteer my own time to help with the excavation, but a whole year went by with no action, and when I inquired about helping out on the dig, I instead received a threatening email, condemning me for exposing a fossil, informing me that they had no current plans to excavate, and threatening civil penalties if anyone found out about the specimen.

It was a bizarre response, considering I could have very easily walked away with the bone, and not a soul would be the wiser, yet we instead went out of our way to contact and alert the proper authorities. We were sitting here, trying to abide by the law that claimed to want to preserve our history. While the authorities were essentially telling me to forget I saw anything and let it be destroyed by time.

It was frustrating. Yes, the bone had survived for millions of years, but the land hadn't been eroded this far down for millions of years. We found it because it was literally sticking out of the earth in plain sight, if you knew what to look for, and now that the land had eroded enough to reveal the bone, the bone risked being destroyed by people or the environment. My rebury job would only protect it so much from those things, considering the lake would flood and recede again and again every year.

Not surprisingly, the government programs built to protect our history—specifically the laws pertaining to not removing artifacts or fossils from public land—was likely to be what allowed so many artifacts and hints to our past to get destroyed. I thought I was doing a good thing by taking the proper legal channels, but instead, I was just condemning this lost soul to be destroyed by nature.

But despite this future disappointment, at the time, I was walking on air, and these much later problems weren't invited to the celebration.

With high fives and fulfilled dreams all around, we loaded up our bikes and finally turned our truck to a new place. Montana had been fun—more fun than my negative biases had expected—but I was ready to get out of there. The land east of the Rockies proved to be as pleasant as it had been the last time I came through, with no one spitting on me for being born in another state. While I still didn't fit in with the country lifestyle, at least I wasn't afraid to talk to people here. I had nearly forgotten that the culture was so dramatically different from one side of the mountains to the next, that they could have been entirely different states.

But still, I wasn't terribly heartbroken to leave. The riding wasn't my cup of tea, and I was tired of the bars and the food options. We left Montana the following morning, and I watched the hills roll by the window. I couldn't help but wonder what perils and secrets lied under the dense wheat that covered every rolling slope.

Those slopes are what kept catching my eye. Slopes that I couldn't ride. My confidence had been shaken, and my relationship with dirt bikes had once again become strained. How was I supposed to conquer such an ordinary and pervasive obstacle when I was still this scared? Was it simply like skiing—a hobby that I accepted I simply wasn't built for? Or was there a way dirt bikes could be ridden within the parameters of my mental thresholds?

Because my hang ups now were all mental, really. My lack of experience and the feeling of not having control in a dangerous situation had started to get in my head and under my skin. While I kept it upright on the last ride and the ride before that, any semblance of ego I had was now crushed under a debatably reasonable fear of downhill. I knew what to do on a street bike on a hill, but I had no idea what technique to use when traction was a distant memory. This kind of terrain was going to take a *lot* more practice.

With my head down, we headed into Idaho, where I was hoping I'd be able to pick up some new skills and start to redeem myself!

It wasn't particularly cold, but I was wearing every layer I could to try to dissuade the biting flies. The bird-sized Montana mosquitoes, however, were not deterred. (Fort Peck, Montana)

The beauty and serenity of camping on the lake was almost inspiring enough to make up for the bugs and the thunderstorms. Almost. (Fort Peck, Montana)

Many of the roads on the official map we got at the museum clearly hadn't been used in the last—I don't know— DECADE. (Fort Peck, Montana)

When it's 100 degrees and you're sick of getting eaten alive unless you wear 8 layers of clothes, you go where the bugs can't get you: In the somehow still frigid lake. (Fort Peck, Montana)

Looks pretty dinosaury, if you ask me. The Hell's Creek Formation that wrapped around Fort Peck Reservoir was as visually impressive as it was historically rich. (Fort Peck, Montana)

Searching for lost treasures sometimes means hiking around where no one else is hiking. (Fort Peck, Montana)

Jackpot. (Fresno, Montana)

We call this a Montana Traffic Jam. (Fort Peck, Montana)

Somewhere between Dinosaur hunting and dirt bike riding, we had to stop to pick up an old car that Hollywood's late cousin had left him. It's stored with his friend, Mark, in Havre until we get round-the-world travel out of our system. (Lewistown, Montana)

We had to get at least one ride in, and the very small OHV park on the high line fit the bill. There wasn't much to see or do, but it made for some pretty pictures. (Glasgow, Montana)

Chapter 11

It was strange coming back to Boise after such a long hiatus. This town was once our home. We drove through our old neighborhood in order to get to our storage unit, stopping in just to trade out some clothing and gear. We couldn't take much more than that, since this time, we were travelers just passing through.

This has been something that's strangely depressing for me as a traveler. Being in a place that you once called home, but having to depend on friends or family in order to exist there. It's something that hurts both my pride and my sense of independence. I know the glass half full perspective is "How great that I've made friends I can count on!" but while that *is* great, my happiness has always been heavily linked to my own independence. When I'm actively travelling, I feel strong and confident because I'm making my way in foreign places. That camp spot I built or hotel I settled into is mine for the night, and I can use it to escape from whatever darkness and social obligations pervade the outside world. But when I'm stagnant in a familiar place, and I can't reasonably support myself on my own two feet, I feel some kind of way about it.

And it's not only that concept of independence either. When I have my own space, I can be the person who helps others. I can arrange my things, decorate my walls with art that soothes my mind, and invite friends and family over for dinner that I cooked with *my* ingredients in *my* stocked pantry. I have the comfort of knowing where I'm sleeping every night, and the freedom to share it if I choose to. There's no hustle to make sure I'm packed and ready to leave at 11:00AM checkout to constantly remind me that this room I'm using isn't mine. In most the world, that's fine, as I don't expect or want to live in most of the world.

But the feeling of displacement you get as a long term traveler is never more intense than when you're in a place that you do still see as home.

I'm not saying it's rational, nor am I saying this need for my own independent space is fair to myself or any of the wonderful people who have given me a place to stay on my travels, but I'm not here to lie about my uglier feelings either. I already admitted to the world I have trust and self-esteem issues and that my dad was a meth addict. Admitting I get sad when I don't have my own home, despite living what appears to be "the dream" life, is mild self-reflection by comparison.

That said, we had a couple reasons to head to Boise, and I was going to do my best to focus on the *good* things about coming back to this place. One being the riding that I was too novice to ride back when we lived here previously. And the other was to get some new tires. Prior to the pandemic end of the world, we had secured a tire sponsor through Western Powersports for Shinko Tires. I've been running the Shinko 705s on my Yamaha FZ-07 since I first started travelling, partially because they were incredibly inexpensive compared to the race tires I was used to, and I knew I was going to be jobless and on a tight budget on the road. Partially because they were one of the very few dual sport tires that came in sport bike sizes (my FZ-07 has the same rim size and width as a Yamaha R6), and mostly because they ended up being great tires that both lasted forever and gave me surprising confidence on any off road we encountered.

My road racer brain was initially unsure about Shinkos, but my ADV brain didn't want to run anything else. So imagine my surprise when we discovered that their US distributor was based about two miles from where we were living in Boise. If that's not fate, I don't know what is, so we headed over and asked if they might support us going forward.

Riding long term is expensive, and while writing books and one-off articles for magazines certainly helps for food, the day-to-day expenses, and gas money, the real perk is that sometimes you can get a little bit of gear for free here or there. I've yet to figure out how any one gets financial sponsorship, short of being Ewan McGregor, himself, and I still end up paying for the entirety of the trip, but if I can save a couple hundred dollars every 7,000 miles for a tire or two, that's a huge help. It's not much, but every little bit adds up on big adventures.

Shinko, much to my surprised, were equally thrilled to be on board for our around the world trip through Europe and Russia. To have a tire sponsor was just about the most exciting thing I could imagine in all of the planning and logistics that go into riding an epic level expedition.

Which is probably why it was even more devastating when COVID crushed that dream and compromised every working relationship I might have had. But the guys at Shinko were understanding, and they had offered to outfit our dirt bikes for this Plan B.

We met up with the Shinko representative as he was preparing a flat track bike for the upcoming Sturgis Rally. Much to everyone's surprise, while the whole country's job market had been devastated by the pandemic, the motorsports industry was better than it had ever been. They were barely able to keep up with the demand for gear and parts and tires, with all of the people out blowing their unemployment money on motorcycles and off road toys.

Speaking of surprises, the fact that the Sturgis Rally was happening at all still blew my mind.

I know bikers are often a rebellious sort, so the fact that there was desire for it wasn't unexpected. And the rural United States had consistently been very disinterested in the masks and hand sanitizer ways of the big cities, so having South Dakota on board didn't shock me either. But in a world of government shut downs, I didn't expect anything would be *allowed* to run as normal, no matter what the people wanted.

We considered going ourselves, just because I had never been, but it felt a little pointless to show up in a year where nothing was going to be what it was supposed to be. If I went to Sturgis, I'd want it to be at its best and most true, with all the flat tracking and ruckus that makes it special. I didn't want to go and have to stand six feet apart from everyone I met.

We shrugged off that idea, and thanked the rep for the tires, then we went to a local Motocross shop to get those tires mounted. Pedro, one of Hollywood's old coworkers, was kind enough to put us up for the night, and then we turned toward Sawtooth National Forest.

The drive was short in distance, but long in turns, and a currently *blazing* heat wave had us taking a dip in every lake and stream we could along the way. Fortunately there are a lot of those in Idaho, and fortunately they're all quite cold.

Now, part of the reason we were going to Sawtooth National Forest was because some friends of mine, Ari and Zack, had filmed a video for Motortrend the year prior where they had strapped chainsaws to some off-beat bikes and did some trail clearing. The trail looked like it had a lot of potential to be fun, and it was only right that I go check their work.

A staging area known as Baumgartner was the ultimate goal. However, little did I realize that the

Sawtooth National Forest is quite huge, and the roads aren't particularly well connected, so making our first stop at the pristine Stanley Lake put us a whole day's drive away from Baumgartner. You would think with all of the travelling I do, I would be better at navigating by now, but... nope. Not the case. Most my adventuring is still about as well-honed as a blind bat in a hurricane.

I sheepishly laughed off my mistake, and we pitched our tent in the national forest. Well, first we tried to pitch it in a real campground for once, kind of wanting a bear box and a real bathroom for... lady stuff (Travelling and being born female has its downsides. Quite a few downsides in general, actually, but the biological ones are the worst), but when Hollywood borrowed an electric bike from our neighbor and did a bunch of circle burn outs, a very angry grounds keeper chased us off. This is why we can't have nice things.

I somewhat begrudgingly rerouted to our usual dispersed camping spot down a nearby road, where we still had easy access to the lake, and there was plenty of wilderness to dig bathroom holes (le sigh). Rugged wild camping is still more my jam anyways, and when you're in bear country, sometimes it's better to be away from the large gaggles of irresponsible tourists.

We unloaded the bikes and Hollywood built a campfire with the abundance of scattered wood. The one advantage to dispersed camping in the forest is that there's often still plenty of stray sticks and broken branches to work with for free firewood, whereas camp grounds are typically heavily picked over. I always felt a little bit like a rugged, old-school adventurer when we built a fire by foraging instead of just cutting the plastic wrap off a pre-chopped bundle.

Even beyond that, there's a lot of zen that comes from camp fires for me. Maybe it's the smell or the sound or the warmth or just the feelings and memories that those crackling blazes bubble to the surface, but there's little I enjoy more than sitting around a fire in a beautiful place.

The next morning, we woke up bright and early and changed into our gear straight away. I had downloaded a map of the forest on the way, compliments of a sign that had been posted in the National Forest. Avenza Maps was this new and incredible app that the Forest Service was using to upload detailed maps of national forest trails. The paper maps were detailed and accurate, complete with GPS overlays so you could track exactly where you were on all those vague, squiggly lines at any given time. It took all of the guesswork out of the consistently unmarked back country trails, and fears of getting lost or twisted around in the indistinct forest scenery were completely banished. I wish I had heard of this sooner, but now that I knew it existed, I was downloading maps for the entire state.

There was one string of single track listed up in the hills around Stanley Lake. A perfect way to redeem myself from my pathetic showing in Montana. I had to make sure I hadn't completely regressed back into a scared mess after the prolonged trauma.

We made it a couple hundred feet when I found myself questioning my new tires. The bike moved erratically, wiggling about on a fire road that didn't appear terribly wiggly. I stopped to air down some more, which improved the ride a bit, but I wasn't sold on these tires so far.

The constant wobbles didn't inspire any confidence, and I was trudging along slowly until we arrived at the single track trail head. A mountain biker whizzed by us, like a white rabbit leading the way to Wonderland, and we gave chase.

The terrain in Idaho felt much closer to Colorado than that of Montana, with its dense forests, flowing creeks, and rocky climbs. It took a few big rocks and roots to help me readjust to the sensation of bouncing and sliding, but once I had gotten used to my tire's new wobbles, I was rolling confidently for most of the day.

And it was a spectacular trail that was worth adjusting for. A thin line of dirt gave us a tour of Idaho's open meadows, where breathtaking snow-capped hills glowered at us in the background. Better yet, the stream and bog crossings were all covered by adorable, single track bridges, just wide enough to serve as a single file foot bridge. While I've come to love water crossings, something about the sound of knobbies clacking over slats makes riding over a bridge feel special.

It was a nearly anxiety free ride, up until we came upon a side hill segment, where my overactive imagination and my periphery worked together to convince myself that the fallen tree branch that was shaped kind of like an exhaust pipe was actually a fallen motorcycle that had thrown its rider down the cliff. It took a minute to determine that was as ridiculous as it sounds, and the leaves sticking out of the branch helped to banish the thought, but it was a low key reminder that I still had a few demons from the Norwegian Gulch. Side hill might never be my thing.

Otherwise though, I was elated to be riding terrain I enjoyed again. On one hand, I didn't want to limit myself to only mountains and forests, but on the other hand, wasn't it okay to say "I love this, not that?" In the current world of politically correct culture, I felt ignorant if I expressed any sort of preference for any sort of thing, including riding. I wanted to expand my experience, but how much punishment did I have to endure to acquire the tastes?

When I was travelling, for example, I struggled with some of the cultures that felt innately negative towards me. Islamic cultures treated me like a lesser person, tourist towns treated me like a living dollar sign, Montana culture treated me like a liberal hippy who threatened their lifestyle, southern culture treated me like a godless feminist who somehow was also a threat to their lifestyle—There was all this stereotyping going on everywhere from everyone and everything, until I found myself so hurt and dejected that I was doing the same. I would have a bad experience, and then, like any person with built in survival instincts, I would reject it from my life from that point forward. It was some combination of self-preservation paired with past trauma of toxic friendships, where I was so desperate to not repeat my mistakes, that I freed myself from a bad situation by cutting it out completely.

And while the deserts and steep hills didn't have feelings to hurt, I still had this hard wired moment of pause where I had to ask myself: if I choose just one kind of terrain, doesn't that make me a poser? Can I even call myself a rider if I don't ride *everything*? Even things like: if I keep riding my little kid's bike, does that invalidate any skill I've earned, since it's not a *real* bike? Don't I have to "upgrade" to be taken seriously? At what point can I turn off my imposter syndrome and just enjoy my hobby how I want to enjoy it, without worrying about the comments from the peanut gallery?

Writing books and magazines and such, putting yourself in the public eye and offering opinions that may or may not be popular has that innate pressure to live up to someone else's standards, and I realized, even after years and years of proving myself—both to myself and anyone who doubted me—still took a toll on my self-perceptions. I wasn't a perfectionist by any means, but feeling less than enough was still an internal problem that nagged at my esteem, which could be triggered by even the most inane, unreasonable thoughts.

But I didn't want to feel guilty for being picky. The mountains are made for dirt bikes after all, and those beautiful rooster tails of water as my tire split a stream crossing, or those little jumps as my knobs gripped uneven rocks brought me to life. It was the most pleasurable version of dirt riding I'd ever done. I'll never love dirt like I love the exhilarating turns of a road race track, but if I was going to learn to enjoy it, this was how and where and when. At the risk of being called a snowflake, maybe I just needed to stay in this comfort zone for a bit longer before I started introducing obstacles that made me doubt myself.

After a great day through the woods, we packed up and headed down to Baumgartner to ride the trails we had intended to ride in the first place. It was a long drive off a very long dirt road, but when we passed under a bridge with bald eagles soaring overhead, I knew it would be worth it.

We took off to explore the following morning, starting first with what was labeled as a "training area" for beginners. This was a pretty cool concept for a trail circuit. Basically, it was a small section of short looping trails that intended to give riders an idea of what to expect before committing to potentially getting lost or hurt in the wilderness. If I could handle these loops, than I had a decent foundation to work with for what's to come.

But these trails were all… steep hills. Again. Not just steep hills, but steep, winding, rutted hills, with blind turns blocked by tall trees, thick vegetation, and mounds of dirt. Then like a shitty cherry on top, there were pine cones littered liberally throughout, acting like marbles beneath my already unstable tires.

This was a combination of everything that scared me, under the guise of everything I just professed to love. I frowned inside my helmet, while sitting at the top of a crest, looking down at the blind curve below. To barrel down a straight hill was one thing, but a curved one? All I could see was myself picking up too much speed and launching off the turn like it was a ramp. I hated that feeling. Nothing that's supposed to be fun should be *this* stressful. Why did my brain keep doing this? Why couldn't I just be chill and easy going?

I guess I was always kind of uptight when it came to what I perceived as threats my life and well being. Weird.

The funny thing about this situation though, was I'd already done all the climbing, so I didn't have much choice but to commit to it and try to fake my way to survival. With a swallow and a deep breath, I pulled in the clutch and pushed myself onto the roller coaster, while subsequently slamming my rear brake to the ground. It was as though I was giving my bike permission to proceed, but punctuated with a "fuck around and find out," so it didn't get too ballsy.

At the bottom of the hill, Hollywood shrugged as I barreled past him with a frustrating lack of control. These tires and drum brakes did me no favors here.

"This is so easy. What's the hold up?" Hollywood said in a tone that didn't reflect how patronizing the question actually was.

"Everything is easy for you." I rolled my eyes. I wasn't going to explain, yet again, the difference in our experience. But by the sixth loop of the training area, I was more discouraged than ever. I was slowly getting a handle on that specific winding downhill slope, but I never felt in control or like I could repeat those results on a new trail.

Luck is what this was. Every lap I survived was out of pure luck. And let's just say I had a bit of a history with Murphy's Laws that didn't have much faith that luck was something I could consistently rely on.

Another loop, and I sped back to the joining fire road to regrouped at the truck and try to talk my way through it.

The problem here, as has been the case since I first threw my leg over any bike, was that I had no idea what I was doing. I'd succeed and not know why. I'd fail and not know why. I was testing the same techniques and receiving inconsistent results, to the point that I wasn't learning as much as I was just crossing my fingers. And the thing is, there *are* actual techniques beyond being a dumb box of wet hairs who didn't care how fast he went.

But Hollywood, being the master of communication that he isn't, had no idea how to convey those techniques to me either. Everything was so natural to him, that he had no idea what he was actually doing, and thusly couldn't explain the movements to me. And me, being the super newb that I was, didn't know enough about dirt riding rights and wrongs to even know what questions I should ask.

I'd ask how to stay in control, he'd respond with generic suggestions to stay loose and disciplined.

I'd ask if there was a better way to slow down, and he'd shrug and suggest the brakes.

It wasn't his fault he was a horrendous teacher. I'd known this about him for years, so I wasn't mad that he was either. The fact that he was skilled was an asset in a safety kind of way, but it wasn't an asset that I could use for studying.

While I calmed myself down, Hollywood took off to go ride another trail, and I sat on the tailgate of the Chevy where I could stew in my misery for a few minutes. I stared at my little green tractor bike and let my mind wander.

I hadn't even gotten to try the trail that Ari and Zack had cleared, and I at least wanted to do that much before I left. Even if I didn't finish it, I could start it and get my bearings. I didn't want to leave feeling completely worthless.

I waited for a few minutes for Hollywood to return, not totally certain where he had gone. Ten minutes passed, and I decided to take off on my own for a little while. At best I might be able to sort out my head. At worst, I'd just be lost in the woods forever. But I had a map, so I could always hike back. Probably.

Either way, even being lost in the woods was starting to sound better than being eaten by bird sized mosquitoes while sitting on my tailgate, so I started up a trail that was about as wide as a large ATV. Not too narrow. The trail followed the cliff, but the drop offs didn't feel terribly daunting with how much room I had to fuck up. It was pleasant. Easy.

I continued up the road for a good while, wondering if this was the trail Hollywood had picked too. Was it a loop? Or would I run into him? Pine trees lined the path on each side, along with the occasional moss covered boulder or meandering stream that saw fit to cut across the path. Stream crossing after stream crossing, accented with dips and easy hill climbs—I was starting to enjoy myself. I don't know what it is about water crossings in general, but something about getting a little wet on a hot day, splashing around, and that distinct sound of the water breaking against my tires was becoming pure bliss for me. Like creating my own little waterfalls in the wild. I stayed committed over abrupt climbs out of the water, then kept my cool as my tires wobbled on the rocks.

I like this so much. I wish I could like those hills, too. Why couldn't everything be as fun as a stream crossing?

It was about education more than anything, I suppose. Though would they be fun if I knew better? Or just less heart stopping?

As established, when I first got into riding motorcycles, I was the most awkward person to ever pretend she belonged in the saddle. I failed the MSF course, I crashed into a curb, I nearly pitched myself off a mountain—if you've tolerated my rambling through the last three books, you know these stories already, so I won't repeat them all. The first time someone exchanged the friendly, two finger biker wave, I was too afraid to even take my hand off the handlebars to wave back. So to go from sitting at my mom's dinner table and announcing I was going to use my tax return to buy a motorcycle, to my getting enough points in the local race series to bump up to an Expert Race License, to riding my Yamaha FZ-07 from Alaska to Panama and everywhere in between, there was a *huge* amount of study and education that went into getting to that point.

I read books, I signed up for classes, I poured over youtube videos and recorded my rides. I used a lap timer for data to quantify improvement, and I got to the point that riding a bike on the street felt second nature. Ninety-nine times out of a hundred, I could navigate high stress, panic-inducing events with grace and calm, because I knew I had all the tools I needed both in my muscle memory, and more importantly, in my mind.

Riding a street bike is easy now.

A class would have been a great solution, but unfortunately, with the pandemic and all, taking a class for dirt wasn't really an option. Even if it was, I didn't really have the money to blow. In my selectively optimistic heart of hearts, I was still holding out hope that the world would reopen any day now, and I could get back to the round the world trip that I'd been saving for.

So what could I do?

I'd googled a few articles written about the techniques in the past, and I'd gotten heaps and heaps of unsolicited advice from both friends and keyboard jockeys alike, but none of those sources clearly explained the movements you should be making in a concise way. Certainly not in a way that I knew how to parrot in real world situations.

All that was left was… watching videos.

Wait, why *didn't* I watch videos? I've used instructional YouTube videos to learn to DIY just about every vehicle repair I've done in the last half a decade. I mean, I'd watched some Graham Jarvis videos in the past, but his techniques often come off as so far advanced, that I wasn't even in a position to practice them yet. Not only that, but they typically required a larger bike with adult proportioned ergonomics that allowed easy standing and purposeful weighting of the pegs. Those advanced expectations of balance never resonated with me in a useful way.

But why not see if there are any instructors on YouTube who can communicate in a way I *can* understand? Many people may be masters of their sports, but to be skilled and to be able to communicate that skill in layman's terms that anyone could understand were two very different things. When I once took a race school with Ken Hill of "Faster Safer" and Yamaha Champions School fame, he told me that they would try to teach me a skill, and if I didn't get it, he would try to rephrase the lesson until he found the right words that would make it click for me. It might sound simple and obvious, but you would be surprised how many instructors, including championship winning road racers, don't know how to communicate their techniques in more than one way. Just like with my scuba diving instructors in Koh Tao or, well, with Hollywood, a clear, unintimidating explanation was all I needed, and muddled, over-complicated, and dismissive explanations were all I was getting.

It was time to delve into the cesspool of the internet in search of quality. This might be the most challenging task of all.

I flipped a bitch and returned to the truck in one piece. Riding alone, I rode slower and with more caution, but in terrain I was comfortable with, I felt more zen than fear. At times, riding with others gave me added confidence, but at others, it felt like pressure to perform that I didn't have to stress on in solitude. Today, that solitude was what I needed.

Hollywood returned minutes after I did. Somehow, we had just barely missed each other on the same trail. I told him about my needs, and we resolved to get to a place with good enough cell service to watch some videos. I started gearing down and loading up.

As I unfolded the ramp and cleared bags out of the truck bed, Hollywood crouched down on the right side of my bike and started poking at the tire.

"I think I know why you feel so unstable lately." He said flatly.

"Lately?" I cocked an eyebrow. He must have hit his head out there if that seemed like a new development.

"Well, on the bike, I mean. Your tire isn't beaded."

I crouched down beside him and followed his finger. Along about three inches of the rim, on the right hand side of the tire, barely visible unless you were looking for it, the rubber of my tire was, indeed, not beaded. It was just enough to cause problems, but not enough to be visibly obvious from any amount of distance.

I blinked a few times. "My tire isn't beaded."

"Well, that explains why it felt so off." He shrugged.

"Yep." I also shrugged.

The tire *had* felt pretty awful the whole time, but at that point, I had just started getting used to it under the assumption it was a different tread style. To be fair, before we left Boise, we were riding on a tire with torn knobbies and a popped inner tube, so my point of reference wasn't strong. It felt worse than my last tire, but way better than the one before that.

But turns out, my constant "this doesn't feel right!" complaints weren't just idle bitching and excuses. It's almost like I actually knew what I was talking about. Amazing how much a single section of tire not beading properly on one side can affect your whole ride.

I was just mad that I hadn't noticed it sooner, but it was on the opposite side that I sit on when I'm checking or changing the tire pressure, so it wasn't completely insane that I missed it. It was more reasonable to be mad at the shop who hadn't verified proper beading before giving me my tire back…

We wanted to bead it ourselves, but all we had to work with was a bicycle pump, and no amount of plunging seemed to create the pressure I needed.

Back to Boise it is.

The shop was as embarrassed as they should have been, and they corrected the problem in a jiffy using their much more high powered air compressor. The difference was immediately obvious even just when doing a lap through the parking lot.

While they corrected their mistakes, I hunted the depths of YouTube until I found a series of educational videos composed by a group of Canadian trials riders. Using both snarky humor paired with clever overlays that explained techniques in depth and with simplicity, while demonstrating said techniques to varying results in the background, I felt like I had hit a gold mine.

Every kind of obstacle I could think of had a video demonstration with slow and concise examples. It was almost like watching a video game tutorial, where they displayed the proper button combinations on the side, while demonstrating the in game scenarios behind it, and like any proper millennial who was born in the same year as the Legend of Zelda, those sweet combos would translate effortlessly through my fingers.

Some techniques didn't apply to me, as most of the bikes they used were large two strokes, compared to my miniature 125 with a fourteen inch rear and a seventeen inch front tire, but the techniques they suggested were more about what your body was doing and less about the bike itself. Finally a language I could speak!

Well, aside from all the "ehs" and "you betchas."

Now I was stoked to go ride again. Like a kid with a new toy, I was determined to put these new techniques to the test in the real world. So where better to do it than right up against the Great White North, itself, right by Coeur d'Alene and Sandpoint.

One reason I will always love Idaho is the abundance of free, roadside hot springs. (Stanley, Idaho)

I'm not sure what I like more—stream crossings, or cute little moto bridges. (Stanley Lake, Idaho)

I know I talk about the views a lot, but seriously, THE FUCKING VIEWS. (Stanley Lake, Idaho)

Single track has become such a normal part of my riding nowadays, I actually like seeking it out. Especially when it's not following the side of a cliff... (Stanley Lake, Idaho)

Smooth is really a relative term. (Baumgartner, Idaho)

When faced with giving up and sulking or giving it one more shot, I'm finally at the point where I'd rather give it one more shot in dirt biking. (Baumgartner, Idaho)

Chapter 12

Long, long ago, there was this guy named Murphy who liked to make up laws. And like most laws that we neither wanted nor voted for but somehow got passed anyways, those laws became a universal truth of awkward dorks like myself everywhere. So when he said "everything that can go wrong, will go wrong, and at the worst possible time," I can only assume he was writing down his clever little catch phrase while he was stabbing my truck tire with a nail, and conjuring up the itinerary for my coming week.

The only mistake he did make in his sabotaging efforts was that he flattened my tire while I was still in the city, so I had a chance to get it repaired within the day. Jokes on you, Murphy.

Hollywood waited at the tire repair shop, while I picked up some picnic supplies at the old familiar grocery stores. Locked and loaded, we started our drive up North. The drive was scenic but long. We followed the Payette River through the tourist town of McCall, where the abundance of packed white water rafts had more fear of flipping in the rocks than they did pandemics, then we continued further to the not-so-tourist town of Riggins. Our destination still a long way off, and most of our morning having been lost to tire repairs, we opted to camp for the night on the nearby Seven Devils Mountains.

The body was willing, but our beat up old truck was not. Somewhere around 5500 feet, about 1500 feet from the top and several miles into the twisting, single-vehicle-wide dirt road that led to the summit, our truck started stalling. We'd go a few feet, then the truck would sputter to a stop. And try as we might, it wouldn't restart. It wasn't overheating, nor were we out of gas. The old girl had a tendency to burn oil, but we checked it often and the levels were still fine. Air filter wasn't too dirty, and the check engine light wasn't even on. I had no clue what the problem might have been. My instincts said fuel pump, but my heart just said "Ugh."

We hiked around the hill side for an hour or two, entertaining ourselves by looking for fossils we knew wouldn't exist here, while the truck cooled down enough to try starting it again. When the truck was cold, it started without fuss, and we were able to limp to the last open camp spot at the summit.

Ordinarily, I prefer to take care of my issues immediately, be it emotional or mechanical, but it was too late to try to get back to Boise that night, and letting the Chevy rest seemed to be helping anyways. Worst case, we would just be stranded at the top of a mountain, thirteen miles from the nearest roadway, and we could take the dirt bikes out to find help. Good thing we have beat up old back up vehicles in our beat up old vehicle.

The view was beautiful enough to create a pleasant distraction. I didn't really want to think about the ordeal any more than I had to at the moment. Neither of us knew what was wrong, and we couldn't afford major repairs right now. The usual art of "throw parts at it until the problem goes away" was probably what we'd end up doing, though it wasn't particularly financially efficient.

We bounced ideas off each other all night, playing bench mechanic to the soothing chirp of crickets, until we both decided that the most likely culprit was the fuel pump. As much as we wanted to press on, we figured we should probably head back to Boise, where the large city suppliers had a better chance of carrying the parts we needed. Fortunately, having an American truck in, well, America meant even large or uncommon parts were pretty easy to come by. I still prefer imports, but every Autozone in Idaho was stocked with enough bits and pieces to deconstruct a Chevy or three.

The following morning, the truck didn't miss a beat, so much so that I wasn't sure if I had imagined being stranded at the side of a mountain the day prior. But just to be safe, we still picked up a brand new fuel pump to keep in the truck, in case it did fail on us down the line. We had both worked together to replace a fuel pump on this truck back when we had lived in Montana two years prior, so it was a task we both knew how to accomplish.

Although last time we did it properly by dropping the gas tank to get to the fuel pump. Not sure if you've ever had a fuel pump fail with a freshly filled tank of petrol (do they ever fail in any other state?) in a truck with a 34 gallon fuel tank, but if I have to do this shit at the side of the road, I'll be taking a Sawzall to the truck bed.

Anyways, with Murphy's second attempt at kicking dirt on my life foiled, we once again attempted to ride to Northern Idaho, to once again attempt at least one, single day of quality riding with two fully beaded tires and no more vehicle faux pas.

The positive note was that the extra time in Boise had given me time to tear into some more of those dirt biking technique videos and prepare for the ride ahead. Always a way to turn a shitty situation into a positive learning experience. Probably.

So embarrassing story—until now, I was terrified of using the front brake in the dirt. As a learned road racer, I was worried I would tuck the front in these low traction situations the moment I pulled the lever. This belief was compounded by the fact that everyone who has ever given me dirt riding advice, including flat track schools and track day coaches (in regards to when you blow a turn and run off the track into the weeds) told me, over and over again, to never use my front brake in the dirt.

And this is probably okay-ish advice for someone who is learning to ride for the first time *ever* and has *no* ability to modulate brake pressure in a tactful or skilled way. Someone who might get scared and grab a fistful of brake at the first sign of adversity probably needs to get comfortable with their rear brake first in the dirt, since it's such an important tool for managing traction.

But the front brake is a majority of your stopping power, no matter what the terrain is like beneath you. And I have no idea why no one who was giving me advice, including my useless boyfriend, thought "Oh hey, Tiff has been riding and racing and touring on motorcycles for over a decade. Maybe she actually understands the consequences of locking the front brake and can manage pressure properly. Dur hur hur."

But no. Instead, all these knowledgeable people who I trusted all continued to tell me "don't touch your front brake!" in one of those "do as I say and not as I do" kind of ways that not only inhibited my learning, but was straight up dangerous advice, quite frankly. I'll be the first to admit that I don't know what the fuck I'm doing, so how was I supposed to know that everyone else I was riding with was using their front brake to regulate speed on down hills, when they not only neglected to tell me that, but straight up said the opposite. No one thought to update the curriculum after I made my way up the gnarly rock gardens? We'll just chock this up to another instance where I should have sought outside advice sooner.

Most new dirt riders (and even some new street riders, lord help us) will be told this same mantra of "don't touch the front brake," and this is probably why downhill situations are the single most terrifying obstacle for most beginners and even intermediate riders.

If you've been told this before, too, let me tell you, the front brake is massively important in a downhill situation in the dirt just as it is for street. It is *still* a majority of your braking power, and it's likely the reason why every single one of my descents in the past was an out of control fight with gravity with no way to slow down. Video after video showed smooth but firm execution of controlled stops at near vertical descents, and I absorbed every nuance I could pick up.

Now, I had no idea if I could execute these drills as easily as the pros did in the videos, but now that the techniques were in my mind, I was ready to try.

Which was good, because those skills were never more important than when we stopped in Elk City for a couple days of riding.

Elk City, ID is an unexpected gem that I'd definitely return to one day. Even on a weekend, it was nearly empty, and the Wagon Wheel trail was easy and fast flowing and fun. The comfortable shade of the surrounding forest sheltered us from the summer sun, while the trail took us along all sorts of mining history in Idaho. Large rushing rivers flowed by, while prospectors panned and dredged for flecks of fortune in the crystalline water. It was a wonderful and peaceful place.

Now that my tire was beaded properly, the ride was incredible, and my grip had me feeling invincible. We turned off onto what quickly became an ultra-rocky climb to a fire watch station, that I conquered with ease (Though climbing the open, narrow stairs to the top of the watch station triggered a fear of heights I didn't realize I had), then we turned to an "easy" Sunday ride through what was known as the "Nugget Trail."

Wide enough for an ATV and with dirt that could accurately be described as "chocolate cake," the Nugget Trail was quintessential Idaho. We rolled through bushes and trees that encroached on the trail, picking up sticky, hitch hiking caterpillars along the way. It was overgrown, with tall grass and protruding branches, but the green leaves against the black dirt made for a lovely visual. I was having a good time until we came upon our first huge descent.

This was steeper than any of the descents before. It was littered with leaves. It was dark. There were tree roots everywhere, and the trail curved at the bottom, revealing a bottomless cliff at the end of the ramp. There was no room for error or out of control barreling this time. A week ago, I would have either cried... or I would have died.

This was the ultimate test of techniques I hadn't even gotten to practice yet.

I swallowed hard, then I walked myself through every step in my mind, one-by-one. I thought to myself, simply and firmly: "Use both brakes, don't touch the clutch, and let the engine braking of first gear slow you down." I could practically hear the cute Canadian accent whispering in my ear, like a friend wrapping an arm around your shoulder and telling you "it's going to be okay, eh."

Another deep breath, and I spoke aloud. "You know how to ride a motorcycle. You know how to brake. You know what to do,"

This was finally a moment where my 11 years of riding experience, 7 years of track and racing experience, and my obsession with good education all came into play. I could have and should have been a bit more loose on the bars for sure, but my muscle memory and riding instincts had no issue finding the proper pressure point for both brakes as the tires dug loosely into the dense and moist dirt.

With control I never thought possible, I eased myself down the hill, hooked around the switchback, and continued to the next drop. We descended several thousand feet, then we climbed back up a couple thousand more.

My stress was high, but my confidence was catching up with it in small and steady spurts. Every descent, no matter how steep and how rough, I found myself in complete control. My speed, my line, my balance—all of it was manageable. I was able to dodge large rocks or ruts on even the most intense descents, and I was able to control my bike around the cliffs that rested in wait at the bottom of each one. It was do or die, and I was doing.

My tires crushed ticks and branches from fallen trees in the dense forest. My drum brakes squealed and my rear suspension squeaked as I forced my bike to crawl down hills at speeds in the single digits. I was still tense. I was still scared. But I was proving to myself, hill after hill, that there was method to the madness, and all I needed the whole time was for someone to tell me what that method was.

Don't get me wrong, I was still hyper aware, only a few notches of pressure short of white knuckles, and not particularly calm in my mind, but fortunately my hands and feet managed to take me through the full five miles of long and dramatic inclines without pitching me into oblivion even once!

I felt like a fucking hero when the world opened wide at the bottom of the final hill. I gave it gas, letting the ruts act as a rail that could launch me onto the easier, pea-gravellier pastures. If I could have beaten my chest like the bro-est of bros on the way down, I promise you I fuckin' would have.

I skidded my tires over the marble like rocks, then tried (and failed) to wheelie my mini bike out of pure elation. I was laughing in my helmet, in utter disbelief. High fives, hugs, a heavy spattering of "I can't believe I really did that!" and s'mores (in lieu of ice cream—the only acceptable substitute) made up my victory lap. I couldn't believe what I had just done. Never had I seen a trail so intense and steep and terrifying. Yet, I did it. I did it like someone with skill and talent might do it. There were no "Just Tiff Things" in me today. Unless those Tiff things were going to start including winning and adrenaline and fist bumps (Spoiler: Tiff things will never include winning or adrenaline or fist bumps).

I don't know if there is any more satisfying moment in a motorcyclist's life than when they achieve something that they thought was impossible, while joined as man and machine (or woman and machine, in my case, obviously. No matter what some of my friends will tell you).

What an incredible sport. What an incredible place. What a time to be alive!

My heart beats for moments like this.

It's not an adventure until something goes wrong? The old Chevy has been pretty reliable for a truck with nearly 300,000 miles on the clock, but big vehicle mechanical hiccups are always a bit more complicated than bike hiccups. (Seven Devils Mountain, Idaho)

Even with the truck to help us carry more stuff, we still keep it pretty simple at camp. (Elk City, Idaho)

After a few crashes on this thing (not all of which were mine, for the record), a new set of bars was in order. The bike handles so much better when it's actually straight! (Elk City, Idaho)

Lots of logging in Idaho, and that sometimes made a mess of the trail. (Elk City, Idaho)

How do you get Tiff to ride into the deep woods? Tell her there will be chocolate cake. Don't specify that the cake is actually dirt and not chocolate at all. (Elk City, Idaho)

I don't know if I've ever felt more like a champion than I did after conquering the Nugget Trail. Maybe dirt biking really can be one of my things! (Elk City, Idaho)

The views from the fire watch tower were worth the ride, but the rocks to get to the fire watch tower made you work for it. (Elk City, Idaho)

Chapter 13

When they say "you can have your cake and eat it, too!" I think just about anyone who has ever dealt with the consequences of eating too much cake has called bullshit on that statement. So when I was sitting there, enjoying the way that "chocolate cake" dirt felt between my knobbies, imagine how not surprised I was when I learned we had to leave, effective immediately.

No sooner had we returned to cell service, on our way north to ride Sandpoint and meet some of my old friends in Coeur D'Alene, Hollywood got a phone call that put a stop to all of my indulgent plans.

His mom had, rather unexpectedly, decided she wanted to move. She had no specific destination in mind, but all we knew was that she had just three days to be out, and that Hollywood's nearby siblings weren't planning to help with that. So while we were about 1200 miles away, and this was by no stretch conducive to our current lot in life, when your mom needs help, you help her.

As quickly as I had sprawled out on our first hotel bed in a month, my comfort was once again ripped out from under me, and we were driving through the night back to Colorado. I might have been more depressed by this if not for the fact that we found ourselves accidentally passing through the Bonneville Salt Flats exactly in time for Speed Week.

Bright white salt extended across the horizon as far as the eye could see, reflecting the sun back at me for maximum sun burn potential. The paddock was roped off from spectators this year, but each vehicle still lined up at the run way, one-by-one, for their five mile speed run. Dirt bikes are great and all, but racing is still greater, and while

COVID restrictions dampened the paddock experience, watching a veritable land rocket exceed 370 MPH right in front of me was a roaring vision that I will not soon forget.

On a normal year, I would have stuck around to enjoy the after parties and nerd out over the engineering involved, but with the event heavily neutered of fan interaction, we instead left midday to continue our drive towards Denver.

Hollywood's mom was thrilled to see us. She no longer saw me as a dark serpent who was strangling her son with travel, and she was eternally grateful for the help, as we hauled her remaining things into a U-Haul. She didn't have a set destination, but Hollywood's brother lived in Scottsbluff, Nebraska about 3 hours away, so that seemed the easiest short term solution until she could find a new place that called to her.

Admittedly, I was bummed to miss out on Northern Idaho, but it felt good to help out. Hollywood had helped my mom move quite a few times, as she had moved around a lot since I left on my first trip. At one point she left Los Angeles to live in Seattle, but the high cost of housing had her trying out Whitefish, Montana with us instead. Montana was a failed experiment for a number of reasons, most of which involved intense local xenophobia and snow shoveling, so she gave Seattle one more try. When the depressing rains had her going down a dark path, she tried Phoenix, Arizona. When the crushing heat had her rarely leaving the house, she decided to just move back to Los Angeles—the last place she had been happy.

A lot of people hate on California for its politics. Like most places with large cities, it prioritizes the human rights of diverse people over the church, which gets a lot of sneers from the pro-life, anti-immigration crowd. But more justifiably, people hate on the abhorrently high taxes and cost of living, as a growing and extreme class divide chases out anyone who isn't born into wealth. It's something that's become difficult for me to stomach as well. Especially being, as someone who doesn't have wealth, nor does my family, moving back required stomaching rent prices that were closer to 90% of monthly income.

But when you're born and raised there, made lifelong friends, enjoyed endless sunshine, and built your entire life and mindset in that dog-eat-dog, fast paced society, somehow these glaring problems don't feel so important. Especially when trying to leave California is met with intense hatred and bias from people who have never even been to the state, it somehow becomes more desirable to be a small fish just trying not to drown in that big pond, than it is to be the biggest fish in a tiny, muddy pond full of snakes.

I've learned over the years that I'll choose a big, diverse city over narrow minded country living any day of the week, and the eternal sunshine of the southwest seemed like a worthwhile option. Even if I'll never be able to afford to buy property there.

That said, once Hollywood's mom was comfortable and secure, we came to a bit of a crossroads. The original plan was to ride Northern Idaho then migrate into Washington then Oregon then head southbound through California to explore the redwoods and deserts. But now that we were well over a thousand miles from Idaho, it was hard to get the motivation to make that haul back. Not the least of which because we had entered the full swing of fire season, and the western United States were performing their yearly rituals of burning themselves to the ground.

Not that Colorado was faring much better. Smoke had blotted out the sun in the Centennial State, and the skies were a dark brown. Having passed by hundreds of thousands of dead pine trees in our drives around northern Colorado, to say this was surprising would be disingenuous, but it made living on the road a much more burdensome and unpleasant endeavor than it had been when we could breathe the air we were sleeping in. But the fires would likely be raging for months, and we couldn't wait around for air quality to improve.

I was at a loss as to where to go when a good friend of mine hit me up to head south. She and her long time boyfriend were heading to Colorado to poke around Telluride, Ouray, Crested Butte, and the Million Dollar Highway, and she wanted a hiking and riding buddy more her speed. I had scarcely explored any of those places, so I was happy to be her Huckleberry.

The smoke didn't thin in the slightest as we drove down, so much so that the distant mountains through San Louis Valley were impossible to distinguish from the skyline. The world reeked of burning wood, and my sinuses were fighting to keep up with all the ash I was sucking into my lungs. I like a good camp fire as much as the next nomad, but the whole world burning down was a bit much even for my nihilism.

Hollywood dragged us to some weird "alien look-out tower," where people left various bits of trash in the supposed energy vortexes, then I tugged us the other way to the Great Sand Dunes National Park, where half naked thrill seekers hauled in snowboards to ride down the massive piles of soft, hot sand. The majority of the women were in little more than a bikini. The majority of men sported board shorts. And my motorcycle brain just kept imagine the painful abrasion wounds that would come from wiping out on a surface that was made up of billions of tiny rocks. To be fair though, my track record in the sand may have built some internal biases.

Something like twelve hours since departure, we arrived in the national forest outside Mesa Verde, and I was walking around the wilderness holding my phone in the air like it was the birth of the lion king in an attempt to find service. When a little tick of magical satellite energy gave me enough bars to receive a text, I learned… that my friend was bailing on me.

The unbreathable air was a bit unfortunate, but I suppose I've suffered worse slights than being stood up in one of the premiere dirt bike riding areas in the country—possibly the world, honestly (But I'll have to ride more of it to confirm that. The sacrifices I make for science).

I figured we'd just enjoy the local riding on our own instead, but as Hollywood is a man of many bros, another rider very quickly volunteered to fill the hole in our plans.

Marshal used to live in Wisconsin. We actually encountered him on my first 49 States tour in Milwaukee, where we spent time doing some motorbike maintenance with his wife and their three-legged cat. Somewhere in those four years, they had gotten divorced, and Marshal moved back to the State of Many Colors, where he now rode dirt bikes.

He lauded himself as a beginner, which I was excited about. In my mind, that meant that I would have someone to learn with and we could push each other.

But it turned out, as we arrived in Silverton, it was clear that he was one of those fearless beginners who was happy to charge in head first, whether he knew what he was doing or not, without any hesitation or self-doubt.

I encountered this often in road racing, as well. One of those people who is more courage than skill, who flies by the seat of their pants. They generally become effortlessly fast very quickly. Though these people often weed themselves out eventually, as their luck starts to run out and their lack of knowledge starts to catch up to them, typically in the form of about a thousand crashes. Some will laugh off the crashes as long as they survive, and by trial and error will eventually become good riders. Others will give up as they build an army of mental demons and physical injuries that no longer let them charge ahead blindly.

Education doesn't typically make it into the training regime. They'll say things like "Oh I just go faster" or "Just don't be a pussy" as their skill is driven purely on ego and a lack of risk assessment.

I wish I had the mind for that, honestly. And I'm mostly complaining out of jealousy for the hold-my-beer team. It must be so nice to be able to tackle obstacles without being able to vividly picture every single way physics can kill or maim you. To get faster and conquer extreme challenges just based on sending it hard enough, without fretting over whether you'll crash and burn or succeed.

I'd say the whole having medical insurance thing probably helps that undeserved confidence, but I think the ability to never overthink (or think at all, really) is enough of a superpower, that consequences like medical bankruptcy or recovery time wouldn't factor in regardless.

Anyways, so needless to say, our riding skills not only didn't match, but they didn't mesh. Being cursed with being infinitely accommodating, I tried to keep a smile on my face, but the smile never stayed there naturally.

Which was a shame, because I had arrived in Silverton with the hopes of conquering Imogene Pass, an infamous Jeep road that climbed over 13,000 feet. I'd heard mixed reviews on how challenging it was. Some described it as a death defying, high consequence road that only the most advanced riders dared challenge. Others described it as wide and rough, but relatively easy, the only real issue being the power loss you'll be fighting in the thinning air. Which is, of course, more an issue with carbureted bikes, but for some reason, it seemed like a majority of all dirt bikes were, in fact, carbureted. At least any dirt bike I could afford certainly was. Though despite my disdain for carburetors, only one of the bikes in my collection boasted technology more advanced than 1872, and it certainly was not the KLX125.

I wanted to try some other mountain passes first to get a feel for the area though, and our camp site just so happened to be right outside California Pass. Being I was also one of those damned Californians invading Colorado and stealing their jobs or whatever the fuck we were doing to them, this seemed like a good opportunity to bond with the Earth over the irrational hate.

But the problem with Jeep trails is, I found that even *I* kind of hated this bit of California. Rather than be a technically interesting and flowing trail, these roads are composed more of ledges, step ups, and tall obstacles. You know, obstacles that might be really exciting to conquer in, well, a high clearance Jeep. It was a trail made for crawling and dead lifting vehicles over obstacles, rather than a trail made for swooping.

But on my tiny 125 with no suspension to speak of, the bike quickly became more of a burden than a joy. The harsh rear spring meant my tailbone was brutalized by the washboard and rock laden dirt road below, and standing on such a small bike was so awkward that it didn't feel much better. The road wasn't challenging, really. At times, the height of the obstacles was near impassible with my small wheels, but there were typically enough outer edge lines on the wide trails to get around the worst of it. It was entirely possible even at my low skill level.

But it simply wasn't fun. It was rough and exhausting, but it wasn't some joyful puzzle or exciting rip.

The fact that my bike started choking and coughing at altitude didn't help either. I turned around and let Hollywood and Marshal ride off on their own. I wasn't having a good time, and I didn't have the patience to not be enjoying the ride anymore. Call me a snob, but to me, motorcycles are far too dangerous a sport to not be enjoying yourself every time you're riding one, and while I can make allowances for anxiety and growing pains, I know what kind of riding I like and what's just a painful chore, and this fell into a painful chore. If nothing else, I was finally starting to discover my own niche within this niche that was worth exploring.

Not feeling enthused by the high passes, the next day, we opted to head north for some more heavily wooded riding. The only decent loops in Silverton required well over 100 miles in the back country, and my bike just didn't have that kind of fuel range. Marshal and Hollywood teamed up in a misguided attempt to convince me that running out of gas and being stranded wouldn't so bad, as sitting at the side of the road until they could get help would be a great adventure. But if you can believe it, that just didn't do it for me. While obviously compelling arguments, oddly, the sales pitch where only I got screwed and everyone else got to have a great time went straight into the trash bin.

Instead, we took our bikes up to the woods around Ouray. Ouray is a cute and quaint mountain town up Colorado's Million Dollar Highway. Like a majority of said mountain towns in the western United States, it was established for mining purposes, but nowadays, it's more of a tourist heavy gateway to hot springs, off roading, and seasonal ice climbing. We passed by a whole fleet of trucks and trailers that appeared to be full of movie equipment, and the hotels in town were booked to capacity.

Though that was just as well. I'd much rather camp in such a beautiful place, and I couldn't have afforded the hotels there anyways.

Our trip took us into the trees, past a brand new Honda Ridgeline with two brand new Honda 450s in its bed. An ATV with mounted cameras was parked in the background. A sight I hadn't seen since I lived in Los Angeles, where movies and commercials were always being filmed somewhere. It was a welcome bit of home when so very far away from it.

No sooner had we found a clearing we could use as a camp spot, Marshal was out of his truck and unloading, raring to go. It was already the early evening, and I was more ready to pitch the tent and enjoy some tailgate fajitas, but there were two precious hours of daylight left, and he didn't want to miss even one of them.

Truth be told, it was a little stressful riding with someone who was in one-week-vacation mode. Being travel is our full time lifestyle right now, we've learned to slow down, conserve mental, emotional, and physical energy, and not stress too much about moving too quickly. My relationship with time and self-care had changed over the years of road life, until I had found a balance that allowed me to prevent burn out and keep a level of enthusiasm and morale.

But for Marshal, much like when I had had a nine-to-five that consumed my week, he was in the mind to "cram everything you can into your day as fast as you can until you're so worn out you need a vacation from your vacation." Every second we weren't in our gear, he saw as a waste, and the intensity of his drive left me feeling guilty for slowing him down. I understood and empathized with the feeling of not having enough time, but between the bad air quality and the guilt tripping with his disappointment in our lack of urgency, I was swallowing my annoyance rather than getting more excited.

I tried to pretend I was into it for the sake of the team, and I even thought that maybe my reservations about riding non-stop were a depression symptom, and forcing myself to ride even when I wasn't feeling it might help me work through and adjust my attitude, but as we were mid trail with the sun dipping below the trees, and Marshal was still looking at the longest possible route back to camp, I was starting to think I just wasn't compatible with his riding style. I'm as chaotic as the next person, and lord knows I'm a masochist, but I just wasn't into riding off road in the dark on a bike without lights in a place I wasn't familiar with.

To my relief, Hollywood had come to the same conclusion as I had, and he insisted on getting back before dark on a more guaranteed route. He *did* throw me under the bus, by blaming me for his decision, in the way that my guy friends often used "my wife says no" to get out of things they didn't actually want to do, without having to admit their own disinterest to their buddies, but at that point, if it got me the conclusion I wanted, I didn't care. I knew how Hollywood was around his bros, and I knew how rare a moment it was that he'd pick me over impressing them.

Marshal insisted on the long route regardless, and we ultimately just split ways at the fork. He headed off to burn off his excess energy, and we tried to figure out which turns would take us back to the main road.

The trail itself wasn't incredibly noteworthy. It was a deeply wooded environment, littered with rocks and sticks and fallen leaves. Streams rested at the base of every hill, which climbed steeply up the mountain side. The hill climbs were dramatic, but I had a handle on both going up *and* down now. My tires bouncing in the weeds, I felt confident and strong. My wheels splashed through the creeks and narrows, then ejected broken sticks and a flurry of leaves behind me. As we rode along, just the two of us, I began to enjoy myself again, without the stress of trying to not disappoint another person.

Eventually, we came upon one final rocky ascent that wrapped around the dense tree line. I gave it my all to surmount the climb to the main road, and I needed every ounce of that "all." The trail head was so steep, it was invisible from the road itself, lest you crept to the edge and stared down into the abyss. It was just enough adrenaline to get me excited to go back to camp and fucking eat.

Dusk and the hell gnats that came with it were in full swing by the time we were back at the truck. I stayed in my gear while pitching the tent, as though the mesh armored jacket and thin jersey had much chance of protecting me. Actually, it usually just directed the mosquitoes to my face instead of my arms and legs, which was, incidentally, not tremendously better. But at least I was one percent more likely to catch them before they had a chance to bite me, even if that meant periodically slapping myself in the face.

We waited for Marshal to return before starting dinner.

And we waited, and waited, and waited.

The sun had dipped down below the horizon, and the left over light was fading quickly. Hollywood and I both started to worry and began calculating a plan to go try to find him if he didn't return soon. Dirt biking was a dangerous sport to do alone in unfamiliar territory, and in hindsight, we probably never should have split at all. In scuba diving, we heavily preach the buddy system, assuring there's at least one person who can save the other in the event of something going wrong, and in dirt biking I firmly believed in the same. Street biking felt much more comfortably independent to me, as the street rarely was completely devoid of passersby, and the terrain was largely predictable, but in the woods?

Still, he hadn't been willing to compromise, and we didn't want to be out this late. He was a grown man, and had made his own decision, knowing full well the risks. We waited a bit longer, letting a sinking feeling settle more deeply into my gut.

Under the last trickles of sunlight, Hollywood started to gear up, knowing a rescue mission might be in order. He'd pulled on his helmet and fired up the 250 when, in the distance, we finally heard an engine. The feint sound of a Kawasaki KLX300. Marshal rounded the bend, and pulled into camp, out of breath and gushing about the trials of collapsing roads, log jumps, crashes, and high stress. It was around this time that he informed us that he had been doing these kind of solo late afternoon rides for quite some time, riding the forests of the Midwest. Being in over his head excited him, and he loved the intensity of it. I felt silly for worrying at all. And I also felt silly for having believed that he was also a beginner who I would in any way be able to ride with. This very quickly wasn't working at all for me. We weren't a cohesive group, nor were we matched as riders or motivations. My mood dropped further.

The next day, we set out bright and early, to appease the need to get back on the bike as soon as humanly possible. We passed by the Honda truck, where the film crew checked us for GoPros to make sure we weren't filming their top secret new vehicles, and then we skirted off the wide fire road for another one of those narrow, steep entries. I thanked the YouTube gurus who taught me to descend, then we followed some two track into the forest. The trail skirted the mountain, offering stupendous views that were, sadly, heavily obscured by the haze of forest fires. Fire season was a particularly tough time to be homeless, as I was always fighting sinus build up and a dry throat, but being both Hollywood and Marshal were smokers, it probably didn't seem particularly bad to them.

I just choked along, straining, dipping, and dodging in the wilderness. There was nothing otherwise noteworthy about this trail though. At one point I got my tire stuck on a large rock, committing to the wrong line in a stream crossing. But after getting off and having Hollywood help me push myself free, using the clutch and engine and unloaded suspension to try to navigate out of the hole, I resolved to learn how to unstuck myself. On a dirt bike with a fourteen inch rear wheel, this was business as usual.

On the other side of the track, we arrived at a clearing, where the film crew was loading up trailers and side-by-sides with their equipment. The team from Los Angeles had finished filming for the day, and being primarily composed of twenty and thirty something guys, they were more than happy to chat with passing dirt bikers. It was nice to take a moment to talk to some people from my home state. I'll admit that hearing how stoked they were to be out ripping around in Colorado, but also excited to go back to their beautiful beachside homes, made me a little homesick for my old life.

I often feel that way though. While I've taken to a more relaxed style of travel, I still occasionally missed the hustle of big city life. The exciting belief that there are endless possibilities to be had and any career was possible. I guess that's why I enjoyed writing books so much now. To many, my life appears to be this lazy but exciting dream life, where I get to travel and don't have to work a job. But in reality, my life was now an even higher stress hustle, where I put in more hours of work than you'd expect to create stories that might never sell or pay out on any level equal to the time commitment to write them. My average pay for a book was probably closer to a few cents per hour, versus my old life in software, where hustling and working hard actually translated into a livable wage. I still worked hard and often, but the in between seems so much more spectacular than the in betweens of city life and daily commutes that it's easy to not notice how much is still mundane, exhausting, and requires real personal self-care and maintenance to keep going.

I used to be allowed to rest after a long day's work, so when that weekend came, I had plenty of energy bursting at the seams. Now every day felt like an uncertain balance of work and play, where I never really got to recover enough to do either well. I never got to work as much as I wanted to, having not enough money or stability to sit down and focus for as long as I needed, so I shifted to being always "on." Every moment of free time, I was working or I was feeling guilty for not working more.

But because of this, I also had to conserve energy when playing hard, making sure once I was done at the end of the day, I had the mental strength left to pound out a few thousand more words. My desire to give my all to both aspects of my life meant I no longer favored long endurance runs over relaxed joy rides. And riding with Marshal was starting to bring that to the forefront in my mind. I had learned to balance my lifestyle, and it was difficult to ride with people who didn't have to.

By the end of the day, we got back to camp, and Marshal was once again annoyed that we had dismounted while there was still daylight. He took off to ride some more, for fear he might leave an hour of the day at rest, and I settled into my camp chair without the energy left to care.

The thought of continuing this riding relationship for another half a week was exhausting. I was starting to hope he would feel the same and propose parting ways, but I think we were all too externally polite to admit it wasn't working.

My only respite was that we would be meeting up with Chris again soon, so I hoped that would help balance it all again. Chris typically took us on long, exhausting, torturous rides, but he didn't have the pushiness, restlessness, and "you guys are slowing me down so I'm going on without you" attitude that Marshal had that was wearing me out so much.

With Chris, I felt like I was growing and he was trying to push me. With Marshal I felt like a disappointment who couldn't keep up.

Maybe another example of my own struggles with self-worth, but there are some personalities that amplify my worst insecurities while there are others that help me shove them in the background. And now that I was over 30, I had a pretty good handle on which was which. I can't say if I was just too tired and depressed to be around that kind of energy, or if I was just not who he was, but I had little patience left. We went to bed that night, and I hugged my pillow tightly.

My issues likely weren't Marshal at all, to be honest. Rather, the unhappy feelings of my ruined trip and my displacement within my own country, that I had been trying all summer to lay to rest. His presence had my old wounds bubbling to the surface, thinking of all the places I'd rather be, and it was a heavy feeling that I wasn't ready to face right now. Fortunately, the coming ride wouldn't give me time to think on them much. Onward and upward…

I was in awe of these mountains as soon as we stopped to set up camp. But I was less impressed as we started to actually ride them. (Telluride, Colorado)

If epic valleys are what you want though, the mountains outside Telluride won't disappoint. (Telluride, Colorado).

It was already getting late when we started our first scouting of the area. The roads weren't terribly challenging, but the constant barrage of the rough and completely hard packed ground was hell on my bad suspension and hell on my back. (Telluride, Colorado)

They called this area "Chimney Rock." Can you guess why? (Ouray, Colorado)

Ouray was more my style, with dark soil, rocks, trees, and streams. (Ouray, Colorado)

We wanted to take a short cut back, having no clue how long the trail was and knowing that sunset was imminent, but I wasn't allowed to stop long enough in town to download a map, so we were taking our best guesses on which way to go. (Ouray, Colorado)

One advantage to camping at high altitudes in the summer is the tent doesn't cook you alive in daylight. Fortunately, the one way we did get along with Marshal's travel style was in camping. (Ouray, Colorado)

Chapter 14

Crested Butte is a utopia of dirt biking. That's what I was told by all of the tourists who had flown, drove, and rode in from far and wide. From tall mountains to rushing creeks, it was a paradise of challenging single track and wild mountain biking. They held rallies and off road meets there each year, and everyone we encountered had the stoke of a California surfer bro.

Chris had insisted on a nice hotel this time, choosing one that served as the starting point for the Colorado 500, a large adventure bike rally that travelled through the high passes of these southern Rockies. We met up with Chris first thing upon arrival, who had his nimble and much more capable KTM 250 this time (opposed to his more dual sport leaning 525), and we stopped into the charming downtown for dinner. Crested Butte wasn't unlike any other high class mountain town in Colorado. Or any high class tourist town in California. Expensive gourmet restaurants lined a clean and decorated street, with old fashioned, charming lamp posts, and deck seating with views of the surrounding mountains.

Marshal had headed off to meet a local friend, so it was just the three of us, like it had been back in Wyoming and on occasion in Colorado. It felt nice to see a friend who I felt aligned a bit more with what I hoped to accomplish with my riding.

Chris was a very methodical person, between his long career in road racing and his passion for dirt bikes. He was a big advocate of education, and despite being incredibly capable, he was one of the most humble people I'd ever met. He had no ego about his riding, though he easily would have been allowed to, and he listened when I said something was too much. These are things I've come to appreciate in a riding companion.

I have a lot of friends who are brilliant riders, but no matter how brilliant you are in the saddle, being good at something and being able to convey those skills to others are two very different things. Hollywood was an incredible rider with tons of natural talent, but neither the patience nor ability to articulate it to others. Chris was more the type who worked hard and exhaustively to better his skills, thus allowing him to understand the concepts and theories behind what he was doing, and thus allowing him to share the knowledge through words. It was a much easier style for me to relate to than the haphazard "go faster" and "don't be a bitch" that my other companions employed.

We discussed the following day's ride in light detail in between catching up on our last few months in Montana and Idaho. I was eager to show Chris what I had learned since he had seen me last. Riding with Marshal, I had felt constantly judged for being not as advanced or foolhardy as he was, and it had been killing my morale so intensely, that I had to force myself to want to ride at all. But today, I was finally starting to get excited again.

And let me tell you, Chris certainly made it exciting.

Black Diamonds covered every trail on the map that Chris had chosen that day.

"At least there's only one black diamond and not two?" I said with a nervous chuckle. If you don't know how trail designations work from dirt bikes, skiing, or otherwise, basically it ranges from green dots, which are the easiest and most beginner friendly trails, to blue squares, which are the moderate difficulty trails, to Black diamond which are, obviously, the advanced trails. Some places use double black diamonds for the most extreme of the extremes.

So imagine how I felt looking at a Black Diamond in what was thought to be one of the most challenging dirt bike destinations in the country. This was… maybe not what I was ready for. But I suppose we were going to find out.

"There are a few spots…" Chris began, "We'll call them exclamation points. A majority of these trails are no big deal. But there are just a handful of black diamond obstacles that will make you say 'ah ha!'"

I nodded along, pretending that somehow neutralized my nerves.

"But worst case, one of us can always ride your bike for you over these little spots. We won't do anything that will risk injury." He assured me.

That actually did make me feel better. I didn't hope to take him up on the offer, but sometimes it's the littlest securities that bring me inner peace.

The road started out a wide fire road that we could easily have done in the pickup, but a few miles in, rocks began to protrude from the road, creating a slightly more 4x4 friendly experience. We dipped and dodged imperfections created by run off, until we crested a mountain to a wide open lot. A lone tree sat at the cross roads, where we could choose a handful of trail options for a handful of vehicle types, all offering a range of difficulties.

Being on motorcycles, however, naturally our route took us to the single track.

And it was a pretty nice example of single track, at least to start. Rolling hills and expansive meadows brought us back down the mountain, rolling over undulating whoops, and banking through well rutted curves. Blue and yellow wildflowers speckled the overgrown grass, while the occasional rock deflected my tires around the well-worn track. A majority of the trail was little wider than a dirt bike tire, but at the most difficult spots, like the large rocks and stream crossings, there was a bit more leeway.

I was doing fine and having fun. The KLX effortlessly rolled over every whoop and root, and I was cheerfully humming along with the chirping birds and meandering creeks. My tires gripped the rocks and splashed through ice cold water with enthusiasm. It was wonderful... up until we got to that first exclamation point. A series of tall rocks that would be better described as stairs for a giant descended down the hillside before hooking onto a narrow trail below. Chris got off his bike, and he walked it down the rocks with far more balance and confidence than I had. Hollywood tried to ride down, only to bottom out the bike and take a hit to his balls. Good thing we weren't planning to have any kids. I stared at the rocks that were taller than my motorcycle at a total loss.

"This is a walk it kind of obstacle." Chris assured me as he hiked back up to help. We walked the bike down, having to lift and shift it around in places to limit the amount of bottoming out and scraping it did, even without any weight on it. Some other riders on some very trick two-strokes came up behind us, and they opted to walk their bikes down too. I'm sure Graham Jarvis could have handled this one, but the rest of us mortals just took our lumps and got through it.

It's times like these that I sometimes just wish I was hiking instead of riding. The distance I could cover in equal time might be much less, but the risk of injury versus the reward is much lower. Fortunately, the ride continued to put enough of a smile on my face to eliminate those thoughts.

Another mile or two down the road, we came upon a fork. Both directions were black diamond trails, so it didn't really matter which one we did as far as my struggles were concerned. I'm sure I'd be flailing about just as wildly on both.

We took the right fork, which dipped us straight into another stream crossing and up into another one of those "exclamation points." I hesitated for just a moment as a steep slab of slick rock came into view, which was enough to kill the momentum that I very much needed to surmount it. I found my front wheel hopping near vertical up a mid-hill stone step up, while my rear wheel dug itself into the earth as if the rock was a makeshift wheel chock. My expression flattened. I couldn't seem to get my wheels up and over, and as steep as it was, it was just as difficult to back up and try again. With two bad knees, walking down inclines was among my greatest weaknesses. So rolling backwards into a creek crossing wasn't particularly better.

I got some assistance up the rocks, and I vowed that that would be the last time anyone would be helping me on this trail.

Forty miles passed, winding through the Rocky Mountain trails, where we found ourselves at a clearing for a break. We still had another twenty miles to go, and I'll admit I was exhausted at this point. We had run out of water, and the amount of work it took to ride my small bike over so many big obstacles, on this warm, sunny day had me dehydrating quickly. I was only pretending to feel confident when we began remounting to continue.

The first half of this section was technically probably the easiest of the entire 60 mile route, having only a handful of rocks and no longer having stream crossings and only the smallest step ups. But there was a different challenge to it. What it lacked in complex obstacles, it made up for with the dreaded "side hill."

Single track in Crested Butte is barely wider than your tire. And single track on the side of a steep hill, where trees and creeks taunt you from below with threats of pain and injury, is somehow worse.

I was exhausted and dehydrated, to the point that my balance was heavily compromised. My inputs were sloppy, my grip too tight, and my focus too fatigued. While I love my little 125, the bike tends to be a tremendous amount of work when getting over obstacles, often requiring you use your whole body to wrench its little wheels over rocks and steps. My tire wobbled in places where it was critical to remain straight, and my nerves were shaken more and more with every passing mile.

The daunting nature of side hill single track would have gotten me on a normal day, so when I was in a state of poor focus and poorer balance, my stress started to peak. I inched along, using my foot as a feeler against the mountain side. I couldn't stop looking down. I knew I shouldn't, but my peripheral vision wouldn't let it go, and every high commitment hill climb only stressed me more. A few more miles of hyper-awareness and stress and sweating, I rolled down a hill into a wide clearing and practically threw my bike into the bushes.

Fortunately, Hollywood had half a bottle of water left in his pack, and a packet of Pedialyte powder to add to it. Pedialyte or coconut water are the most effective way to survive intense dehydration that I've found, from my "years of racing in 110+ degree desert in all black leathers" experience, and it was the only way I'd be surviving the last ten miles of this ride.

Exposed to the sun and working ten times harder than everyone else, with dexterity compromised and muscles tense, I sobbed into my helmet, a grief made more intense as I knew every tear was water I very much needed. After all, the next 10 miles were supposed to be the most challenging part of the ride.

Eventually, Chris came back to find us. He took pity on me, pulling some extra water from his tail bag. I downed that lifesaving liquid as though I had just crawled across a desert in a bear suit. I'd need every drop for what came next.

Much to my delight, we had finished the section of relentless side hill, and it was now, quite literally, all downhill from there.

But the downhill was comprised entirely of switchbacks, and the switchbacks were torn apart and conquered by massive tree roots. I was dabbing my bike down around turns so tight, they nearly required a pivot turn to keep from touching a foot down. I gave up counting the number of turns after somewhere around thirty. The roots I could take with my feet on the pegs often bottomed my suspension, giving my entire body a jolt with each drop and bounce.

"All downhill from here." I repeated to myself, just so I could laugh at the irony of this torture trail of pain and white knuckling. Another switchback and another. Another root and another. Another rock, another drop off, another jolt to my vagina.

How is this even fun for people?! Why do they do this to themselves?! Would it be that much easier if I was on a bigger bike? Had bigger wheels? If I could stand up and maintain stability? Was my little mountain goat of a motorcycle finally becoming more of a hindrance than a treat?

I couldn't say. But I *could* say that this was one of the most grueling 60 miles I have ever put myself through in my life. I crawled along, being outrun by the snails and other slow creatures that don't even have legs, until the gods of speed and mercy opened into a wide creek. A well-built bridge that was only as wide as my handlebars, stood before me. A wide open clearing sat on the other side. And the road back to our truck was just thirty feet above us.

"I made it!" I practically screamed, no longer worried about expending my remaining energy. Sure, I still had to ride the fire road back to the truck, but it was a fire road! It was flat and smooth and just a little gravelly. I could probably even hit 30 or 40 miles per hour. SALVATION. FREEDOM. SUCCESS.

I laughed until I nearly cried, I fist bumped my companions, and I took in the beautiful view of the mountain we no longer had to climb or fall off of.

And then I got back on my bike and rode over to the trail to get up those thirty feet to the road.

The incline shot straight up. It was built by giant stone steps, held together by narrow paths of mud. It was a mess of the gnarliest, most upsetting shit I've ever seen in my life. The final and largest exclamation point of them all.

While in my gut, I wanted to scream "WHY?!" before promptly throwing my bike in the creek and walking home, in my brain I was so incredibly angry that the worst part of the trail had the *audacity* to be right here, at the very end. It laughed in my face, dangling a carrot of comfort, happiness, and ice cream.

No.

Fuck that shit.

That is not okay.

I pointed my front end at the only possible line that my little bitty tires had any chance of traversing, and I twisted the goddamn throttle. I wrenched my bike over one rock, then dug into the hill side, narrowly catching an edge that let me skirt the largest of the rocks. I was fractions of an inch from slipping over the side, and if that was to be my fate this day, after all I'd ridden through, it would have had to fight me tooth and nail and sprocket to fulfill that destiny. With all of the anger and frustration and depleted patience I had, I threw that bike up that godforsaken climb, and I tore off down the fire road to safety.

Crested Butte would not win that day. I had been through too much. I wanted ice cream, and I wanted the fancy hand churned kind with the peanut butter cups. This was not negotiable.

Honestly, I'm not sure how I got over that last hill that day, but in light of everything else I had rolled over throughout these travels, I suppose it seemed par for the course. It was as though I got to the point where I was so tired, that I didn't care anymore. I couldn't even register anxiety. I could only register "this is all that stands between me and my goals. Me and victory. Me and a comfy bed and a cold glass of ice water."

And maybe that's all it takes sometimes. Just wanting something more than you have the capacity to be afraid of it. In the earlier instances of bad obstacles, I had people to rely on and people who could save me. I had the mental capacity left to process fear, and the hydration to consider the option of more physical but safer options.

But while staring at that mud and rock wall on my wits end, all I had was myself. Just like when doing long distance travel on these big, round-the-world journeys that we do, you learn to trust in your abilities even just the smallest bit, and in the times that come to test your mettle with the roughest moments of stress and exhaustion, you know you have no choice but to step up to the bat and swing with everything you have. You're exhausted and you don't want to, but your survival instincts won't let you make any other choice.

And that was where I stood in Crested Butte. I would conquer it simply because, in that moment, I had no other choice.

I didn't get my ice cream that night, but I got incredible sushi. That's a compromise I was willing to make.

The single track was certainly very singular, leaving very little room for mistakes or deviations. Especially once that single track started following some side hill. (Crested, Butte, Colorado)

These riders showed up on two $30,000 dirt bikes, fully built by professional endurocross racers. Needless to say, they were pretty surprised to see a $1000 KLX125 in the middle of their trail. (Crested Butte, Colorado)

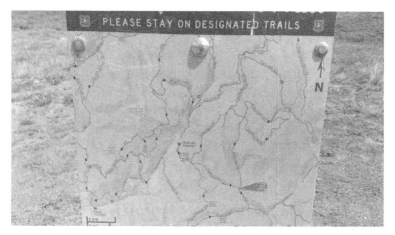

When you're choosing a route, and all of them scream death. (Crested Butte, Colorado)

Just finished 60 miles of black diamond single track in the Rocky Mountains! I'm a hero! A god among bikers! Nothing can stop me!

*Glances at final 30 feet to the trail

Whelp, I'm just going to go cry in the corner. Don't mind me. (Crested Butte, Colorado)

Chapter 15

We weren't done with Crested Butte yet, though I woke up the next day feeling as though I had carried my bike through a marathon. But Chris had another trail he wanted to show us, and well... once the adrenaline kicks in, you don't really notice the pain of existence anymore, so I would manage.

We staged in the same area as before, but this time, instead of taking the single track by the tree atop of the hill, we took a wide UTV road. A routine high elevation storm the previous night had soaked the mountainside, and deep red orange puddles speckled every imperfection in the trail (and in Crested Butte, there are only imperfections). We rolled along, taking creative lines to sweep around flooded whoops and felled branches. It was unexpectedly delightful after the prior day's torture fest.

My knobbies left a sweeping impression through the deceptively grippy mud, and I felt great when we stopped for our first water break.

"I've done this trail before," Chris told us, "several years ago when I was younger and more reckless."

I laughed nervously. *Here we go.*

KTM had held an event in these mountains a few years back, offering demos and trail rides with some factory sponsored KTM riders. Andrew Short, himself, was leading the ride.

Andrew Short was an obvious pick to lead the advanced ride, having competed in everything from the Baja 1000 to the Dakar Rally. Chris, feeling confident, approached him to talk about maybe coming along.

Now, while I have all the respect for Chris's riding ability, as he tends to make even the most violent rock gardens look like he's skipping through a field of flowers—unlike myself, who would skip through the field and trip on a rock, then somehow manage to face plant in an inconveniently placed thorn bush. No, he was the kind who would spin around all Gone with the Wind and shit—I can understand why riding with a rider with Andrew Short's riding pedigree might be a touch intimidating.

Which is likely why he approached Andrew Short, and he asked with tentative confidence if it would be okay if he had to turn around if he came upon something over his head. Short assured him that would be fine, then they were off with a group of the best of the best. All was well and good, until they encountered the obstacle that we would come upon next...

"What kind of obstacle was it," I asked, trying to imagine what kind of horror movie, life-destroying hell scape would have Chris turning back.

"You'll know when you see it." He responded with a grin.

My inner masochist gave him the two finger guns and a "hell yeah!" My inner clumsy, bumbling dufus rocked in a corner in fetal position. I've seen enough of Crested Butte to vividly paint a mental picture of an epic mess of what-the-fuckery. I won't say I was ready for it, per say, but I was ready to be horrified. Dirt biking was really just a constant exercise in "But wait, it gets worse!" for me so far, so if nothing else, it may as well remain consistent. If anything, at this point, I was about ready to yell: "Go on! Impress me!"

I settled onto my banana seat, contemplating my life choices while kicking my bike back to life. With a roar and a rumble, we were off into the trees.

The road narrowed only slightly. It was still wide enough for a UTV, but no longer wide enough for anything larger than that. We weaved around water filled pits and splashed through others, finding nothing of particular challenge. And then we happened upon the "feature" Chris had been talking about.

Uphill, surrounded by tightly packed trees, was a field of boulders, held tightly in place by the earth. It was a sight that made eyes sore. And a ride that would make my ass sore. The rocks were large and smooth, but so densely packed, uneven, and plentiful that there were no good lines. There weren't really lines at all. Just a series of insurmountable stones that threatened to throw you into another stone.

"So at this point," Chris continued his story. "I was ready to turn back. I went to Andrew Short and told him my plan, and he just shook his head.

'You can't turn around,' Short said.

'But you said—I'

'I lied. You can do this.' Short insisted again.

As you can see, this wasn't the most inviting obstacle, yet, with no other option I decided to give it a try. And somehow, I made it to the other side."

"It's definitely something." I chuckled sheepishly, as I rolled my tires into a rare flat spot, in between some tall tree roots.

"Do you want Hollywood to ride your bike up?" Chris asked with concern.

Did I? Would that have been easier? Was I better off on my feet or my wheels? Was it really *that* much worse than Wyoming? Hell, than the day prior?

I asked myself all of these questions on the inside, but on the outside, that manifested in a shrug.

Rocks were kind of my M.O. at this point. My mind and body had finally gotten used to the sensation of deflection and bouncing around. They were used to getting stuck and working together to leverage both the power in my legs and the lack of power in my engine to tractor over the worst of it. This was just another day in the life compared to yesterday's sixty miles of single track and side-hill.

"No, I think I've got this." I replied, my eyes still fixated on the field before me. I scanned the rocks, picking out shapes of different boulders, imagining how it might deflect my front tire. For the first time, my overactive imagination and oft overwhelming anxiety actually felt like a super power, where I was able to build a ride-able route based on calculated assumptions. A clear line formed in my mind. Zig here, zag there, hard right, hug the tree, skirt that step up, leverage that root, duck under that branch. There was a way through here, even on my itty bitty bike. It was just going to take planning and creativity. And my nerd brain actually has a pretty significant stockpile of both those things.

I bumbled through the rocks best I could, trying to execute the line that seemed much easier in my mind than it was with real world physics. I was thankful for my little bike that even my meager arms could muscle around. My calculations weren't perfect. Rocks on the trail often end up larger than they initially appear, and it wasn't long before I found myself spinning my rear wheel, stuck in a pit between stones.

Now, this has been a constant issue for me that just about always required me getting help from one of my riding companions. That is to say, moving too slowly

221

through big obstacles, and consequently getting my rear wheel stuck without any of the momentum that I needed to free it left. I would typically dig my wheel in and make it worse, before I would dismount in defeat, and Hollywood would come over and have to help push me out.

But, much like when struggling with the downhill in Idaho, getting stuck on the rock the day prior, in front of everyone, feeling like a terrible burden, I decided it was about time I learned to dislodge a stuck wheel properly, too. While everyone else rested, I spent the previous night watching videos on techniques for this exact situation. Little did they know they were going to wake up next to a 1% competent dirt rider.

So, what I learned was that there are three common ways to fix this situation, where your front wheel is sitting on the other side of the obstacle, and your rear tire is just digging a hole.

First, there's the run up technique. Essentially you're going to back up the bike as much as you can, then try again to give it throttle and use momentum to get your rear wheel over the obstacle. Typically you're only backing up a couple inches, and sometimes those inches are enough. I tried that one. It was not enough.

The second technique is a solid tractor methodology. It's a… dump the clutch kind of technique. Basically, you're going to try to press your weight back as far as you can, in hopes that more weight on the rear wheel will provide extra traction. Then you're going to pull in the clutch, rev up your bike, then dump all of those RPMs into your drive train at once, giving your bike the ability to surge itself over the obstacle.

This… almost worked. But still not so much.

The last technique involved more of a bounce. You would essentially unload the suspension and bounce your rear wheel over the obstacle, using a combination of the first two techniques. Basically, back up as much as you can, hold in the clutch, load the suspension with your body weight, rev the engine, then release the suspension and the clutch together, so the bike rebounds and surges forward at the same time, giving you both a bounce and torque to try to get out and over the obstacle.

That was the ticket! I used my legs to help leverage the bike forward, and the bike wrenched itself free from the pit. I cheered aloud. This was the first time I ever pulled off the technique, and it worked just as the videos had said it would! I couldn't believe it. Again, in all my struggles, all my feeling worthless and incapable, the reality was that I could get through any of this if I actually knew the technique needed to perform the tasks at hand.

I'd been riding motorcycles for years, and I understood how all the controls worked. But I didn't understand the first thing about how to use those controls to conquer complex obstacles. So as I added these little techniques to my repertoire, I finally started to feel capable.

Riding a motorcycle is a complex art form of very specific inputs that use physics to conquer different terrain. So while I'll always envy the send it crowd, who make zero effort to understand the actual science behind the techniques they've learned through luck and trial and error, as a nerd who loves to geek out over every minute detail of my hobbies, this was not only extremely satisfying to see the theory working in execution, but it took so much of the fear out of riding dirt when I knew there was legitimate rhyme and reason to what output my inputs would return.

To everyone's surprise, I used my newfound skill and my careful line to my advantage, and in moments, I was atop the boulder field, feeling like a champion.

Well, up until I looked back at my companions to throw up a fist pump, only to hit my helmet into a low hanging tree branch, consequently stalling the bike. No amount of skill makes Tiff less Tiff, I suppose.

Chris approached me to give me a high five. "You did it!"

"Fuck, I guess I did!" I laughed to myself, as though it was no big deal. But it was a big deal to me. It was huge, actually. It was a moment where I was legitimately proud of how far I'd come, and I had a quantifiable result to show for it.

The rest of the ride was much like the start, mostly composed of undulating puddles and the occasional root. Nothing compared to that several hundred meter rock garden. We continued higher and higher, until the altitude was coming in at about 11,500 feet. Further still, down a steep dip, a deep puddle, and then straight back up again, we found ourselves at the bottom of one last incline.

The incline was as steep as it was loose and rocky. And atop the incline, at about 12,000 feet, was a solitary flag pole. Stars and stripes waved violently in the vertical distance, while threatening black clouds collected overhead.

Storms in these high elevations can come on quickly, and to make matters worse, they were heavily prone to lighting. It was... really not the time to be visiting a metal flag pole. But we were too close to turn back, I thought.

Just a few hundred more feet and we'd be there.

Hollywood and I looked at the hill, we nodded to each other, then set our eyes forward. It was tall and it was long and it was loose and it would require all of our commitment. Commitment I now had. I twisted the throttle, and I was off.

My little tractor started strong, plowing through the loose rocks with a hungry vengeance, while pushing through the oppressive forces of gravity. One hundred feet, then two, higher still, and then...

My little bike started to choke. Momentum was falling off fast. I feathered the clutch and revved hard, trying to keep the RPMs up so it wouldn't stall, but my bike returned only a light cough. The KLX125 sputtered and sobbed and gave in, with just 200 more feet to go. Apparently riding vertically up a hill at 11,800 feet was my sea-level-tuned carburetor's absolute limit.

I stood sideways on the mountain, staring at the top, with a lead weight between my legs.

Hollywood made it another twenty feet or so. He jumped off the bike and tried to combine revving, clutching, and running the motorcycle to keep it alive. But the steep incline made it impossible for him to push it fast enough to keep it rolling. A pronounced silence fell upon the mountain as his bike stalled out, too.

11,800 feet for the KLX125. 11,820 feet for the KLX250. Well, at least we can say we found our limits.

We both sighed. We looked at each other. Then we both laughed.

Maybe we could have rolled back down and given it another try, but with the storm coming in at an imminent speed, there wasn't much point or logic in that. And honestly, while I was laughing on that hillside with Hollywood, I didn't even care.

No, I didn't need to see the flag. I was completely happy and content with everything we'd done already.

I got some help turning my bike around on the hillside, and not wanting to try to kick that thing to life in these circumstances, I used the momentum of rolling down the mountain with the clutch pulled in to bump start the bike to life.

My little bike fired up as we descended back down to 11,500 feet. We rode back out the way we came under the large rain drops of the beginnings of a high elevation storm.

Somehow, going back down the gnarly rock garden was easier than coming up, and I made it through without even touching a foot down. I felt powerful, skilled, and strong as we rolled around the gentle, twisting fire road back to the truck. I hit a good rhythm and I was going faster and riding more confidently than ever. It was a road I had ridden four times now, in and out and in and now out again, and there's something to be said for riding the same trail more than once.

Up until now, nearly every single ride had me in a constant state of reacting, always having to read the trail for the first time. I had to figure out how to traverse each new obstacle as quickly as they came at me, anticipating what might come next, how I would be able to conquer it, and how to survive the day. I scarcely got to repeat the same ride twice, which meant I never really got to build any sort of speed or confidence.

In road racing, for example, riding the same race track over and over and over again until you know every turn that's coming up, where the apex is, where your brake markers are (*cough*where the bumps are*cough*), and exactly how the asphalt slopes and tightens, is integral for getting faster. Some people can read and learn a track layout faster than others, but no one is their fastest on the first—or even the third—time there. And this isn't simply because knowing a track lets you anticipate the turns that are coming next, but because knowing the turns means you don't have to expend mental energy on them. You can focus 100% on what you're doing to control your motorcycle. You have the unique opportunity to focus completely on yourself, try different techniques to see what works and what gets you through the turn faster and safer and more efficiently, which you can't reasonably try when you're actively having to read the terrain, road conditions, and hazards at the same time that you're riding over them. You can't build your skills in a meaningful way if you never repeat the same tracks.

Maybe this dirt bike boot camp of hardcore riding has put me at a bit of a disadvantage in some ways, as I never get that chance to get comfortable in a consistent environment. I'm always in a state of hyper-awareness and hyper-vigilance, trying to survive the unknown death traps that could be around every corner. I'm building skills, yes, but I'm never able to relax while doing so, and relaxation is so important to implementation. I don't retain panic decisions anywhere near as well as I retain intentional decisions made in comfort. One is instincts and reaction, while the other is thought and knowledge.

One day, if I'm ever able to settle down somewhere so I can have comfort and consistency again, I hope to find some nice trails I can learn to flow on more regularly.

When we got back to the truck it was high fives all around. Hollywood was proud to see me going so fast, and I was proud to see myself feeling so elated after a day of hard riding. This is what dirt biking is supposed to be. Or all riding, really. Overcoming challenges, personal accomplishment, high fives, and laughs with friends afterwards. Whether it goes well or poorly, those are the things I crave most when I ride. Both the personal satisfaction, and being able to share it with passionate, like minded buddies.

That's what I crave most when I do anything really, be it bikes, hiking, travelling, camping, or even writing books. It's growth that gives me purpose, and it's sharing and exchanging stories of that growth with others that gives me that much more.

I love riding so much. This was almost worth having my whole life plan ruined by a global pandemic.

Well almost. But I sure felt like a rock star right then.

That night, we returned to the hotel and laughed among each other while watching videos of the Erzberg Rodeo, all of us feeling a little bit like Graham Jarvis after that rock garden.

The next morning, as we determined if we should stay to ride one more day or head out for the next location, Hollywood got a phone call that made the decision for us. His sister needed some help in Denver, so with goodbyes and thank yous passed around, we took off for a couple more days in Colorado, recovering physically from a long week in the southern Rockies. The trip had started a bit rough, but it ended so well that I was riding high the whole long drive over.

But after a few days of rest with Hollywood's sister, the next question was, naturally, where do we go ride next? I looked at the date and I looked at the map. It may be a pandemic, but with a friend's birthday coming up, it seemed like a reasonable enough time to go back to California. There was a lot of riding I'd never gotten to do there, and it was about time we see some of my own friends for once. I'd barely seen my race family in the four years since I'd started dating Hollywood, and I knew with the pandemic being what it was, I likely still wouldn't be able to see most of them, but if just one or two people were willing to exist within 6 feet of me with their helmets on, it would be worth the trip.

With over 1000 miles ahead of us, we started the long ride home.

Flag Mountain sounded neat, but stalling 200 meet from the top while a big storm lingered over the horizon made it another destination for another time. Successfully bump starting my bike on the way back down, however, made the attempt a victory regardless. (Crested Butte, Colorado)

The views of the Rocky Mountains never got old. Riding dirt bikes really takes you to some new heights that I'd never have gotten to without one. (Crested Butte, Colorado)

Chapter 16

The last time I came back to California, it was March and I was getting my Russian visa to ride around the world, only to have COVID ruin everything.

This time I came back to Los Angeles to ride dirt bikes with my friends, only to have mass forest fires shut down the entire national forest system of California, just because some idiots decided their gender reveal party was more important than the entire ecosystem.

I think this is yet another sentence in the definition of "Just Tiff Things."

But one day before everything had shut down, I fortunately managed to sneak in one single ride.

The drive back to California was uneventful, hauling straight from Denver to Orange County. We spent a couple days celebrating my best friend Joe's birthday, then when the weekend came around, we headed north to meet my hard enduro obsessed friend, Stacy, in Lancaster.

It was the beginning of September, and temperatures were still high in the deserts. But being California is always only a few hours away from beaches, deserts, or high mountain forests, we had some options to get away from the scorching sea level temperatures.

Feeling confident and strong, I didn't bat an eye when Stacy suggested we ride a trail called Gold Mountain in Big Bear.

"It's a lot of rocks." She said.

"I've been riding in the Rocky Mountains all summer" I said.

"We can always turn around if it's too much." She said.

"How hard could it be?" I said.

In hindsight, I already knew that 'we can always turn around' is bike-speak for 'chances of dying are impressively high,' but 'chances of dying are impressively high' is also bike-speak for 'It's going to be extra rad when you survive,' so I wasn't about to be the wet blanket.

Besides, Stacy was a mamma bear type in general when it came to riding. She was the kind of person who would encourage you always, never make you feel like a burden, and offer enthusiasm and support if things got tough. I'd go so far as to say she was the person I wanted on my team when *I* wasn't even on my team. Knowing this, I felt confident committing to whatever road she decided we could manage. She trusted me when I asked her to ride down to Mexico with us a couple years prior, despite not being a street rider. So I trusted her when she invited us to Gold Mountain, despite not being a dirt rider.

We loaded up the truck first thing Monday morning. Smoke was thick enough to color the sky in a dark green and brown, but as an almost blessing, the thick black blanket provided the slightest relief from the heat of a Southern California summer. I couldn't breathe, sure, but at least I was mildly not hot while I was choking.

Stacy would be riding her KTM Freeride, a lightweight 250 2-stroke that was built for conquering the hard stuff. We were on our usual overweight KLX tractors, but what we lacked in suspension and weight savings, we made up for with torque and low gears, so surely it would be fine. We loaded up all three bikes, and a few hours later, we were unloading in the National Forest of Big Bear.

The ride started easy, down a deceptively rough fire road, where the sun-bleached earth hid the occasional dip or washboard. We flew over the road with ease, and arrived at the Gold Mountain trail head in short order. In front of me was a hill covered in loose shale, up a moderate incline. Nothing noteworthy. I opened the throttle, and my 8hp engine braaaped right up.

"Is that what you call rocks?" I laughed, feeling both a little cocky and excited. I figured this would be easy.

"Oh, we've only just begun." She grinned back.

One switchback, then two. My bike rolled into a deep whoop, and the suspension unloaded as we popped up the other side. I chose a careful line around a rock ledge, then climbed through more shale. I was feeling like a badass as I navigated the rocks. Though some of the dips and step ups were so sudden and deep, I remained reasonably cautious that it could still get worse. There was definitely a challenge to be had here, but I was riding with one of *my* friends finally, and I was too excited to worry. Sometimes just knowing you have a legitimate support system out there is all I need.

"You have great clutch control." Stacy noted, as we stopped at the edge of the trail for a water break. She pondered for a moment, then addressed me again. "Yeah, you should be fine."

An odd statement so far into the trail, I thought. We'd already done some solid inclines, and the trail was only supposed to be about 3 miles, so I couldn't imagine it getting much more extreme.

Which is a wonder, because I would have thought my imagination was smarter than that by now.

Sometimes I wonder if any of my decisions have gotten smarter, really. I don't even have any concussions to blame for this lapse of judgment. I shook it off and continued on, bright eyed and determined.

And then around the bend, I started to understand what she was getting at.

I stood staring at the next stretch, so dumbfounded, I couldn't even begin to dissect the best possible line. Before me was a set of rocks and ledges that would have had me scrambling on a hike. On my seventeen inch front and my fourteen inch rear tire, we were going to be performing some miracles.

So I took a deep breath and I looked for the puzzle. A good rider on a good bike can likely surmount most obstacles on piss and vinegar alone. But a newer rider like myself, with self-preservation instincts and suspension built for a child holding me back, would have to approach this kind of obstacle with careful analysis. My eyes scanned the rendered earth before me, and my mind began to build a route.

Up that rock, behind that tree, tight right over that boulder, and sudden left across that ledge. Follow the bushes, where the dirt is more gradual.

With the route planned, I set out to execute. The dirt behind the tree was a bit softer than I imagined. My clutch control saved me when my wheel neared the edge of a ledge. But I felt like a hero when I arrived on the other side.

"Whoo!" I exclaimed. "It can't possibly get harder than that!"

Stacy just smiled.

Fuck.

What did I get myself into?!

It's... it's only three miles. It'll be fine.

A few more puzzles, and nothing was stopping me. Then we arrived at the crown jewel of Gold Mountain. Finally, I felt like I had been clued in on the joke. I stood in awe as a field of jagged boulders rested before me. They were loosely piled atop each other. No mud or dirt had sealed them in place like they would have been in Colorado. No, this was a pile of perilous dread.

A Jeep crawled over the boulders in the distance, clanking each rock together with a sound that resembled breaking glass. The rocks moved and shifted under weight and power, while also reaching upward and threatening to grab any low hanging axels.

Without a second thought, Stacy stood on the pegs of her Freeride, and with the skillful weighting and de-weighting of the balls of her feet, she rolled right over even the most heinous of rocks, playing a melody of shattering glass and two-stroke behind her. Hollywood did the same, (though the KLX sounded a bit more like a sewing machine).

I got stuck on a big ass rock.

Fortunately, having now practiced the techniques of getting my rear tire wedged on big ass rocks, I had a trick in my hat. It was like the whole summer was just preparing me to survive Stacy's extreme day rides. I started out by trying the "run up," where you back up enough to try again to have enough momentum to get over the rock. But the rock was big enough that I couldn't back off of it. So I tried rocking the bike free, while trying to time a bounce and clutch dump to get over the rock. Still stuck.

So I got off the bike and kicked the rock out of the way. That did it. Sometimes primitive problems need primitive solutions.

With minimal drama, I made it over the rest of the boulder field, occasionally wrenching the little wheels over miniature mountains, while getting extra *extra* practice at those run up and bounce techniques.

"Wow!" I exclaimed. Or at least I would have if there was any breath left in my lungs. "I can't believe I made it."

Again, Stacy smiled.

Again, my soul quivered.

But on the other side, the final obstacle rested before me. It was still a field of boulders. It was still loose and wild. But this time, every obstacle had been combined into one. It was step ups. It was rocks. It was ledges. It was inclines. It was dramatic whoops followed by narrow lines. And it was towering switchbacks that snaked around the trees. A game demanding not just clutch control and line choice, but momentum.

Blind momentum, as you couldn't see the hell scape around each corner until you were hooking through a tight mess of clanking stones.

I might have suggested this be the point where we turn back if I didn't know what 'back' looked like. I pondered what was worse, and both came up with equal pros and cons.

Hollywood stood beside me, looking up at the trail with the same kind of shock and awe. Then he turned to me and placed a hand on my shoulder.

"What if we add whipped cream and a cherry on top."

"Done."

Much to my surprise, with a combined effort of run up techniques, KLX tractor gearing, extremely careful line choice, (a few clumsy drops), and occasionally using my legs for extra leverage, I dragged that bike up a trail that was not fit for human traversing.

And on the other side, we were rewarded with an easy, rocky descent. Stacy assured me that was all, though I was now constantly in fear that it might suddenly have one more obstacle. But before I could savor that reward, I signaled to stop for some water. In the heavy smoke, I found myself hacking up an excess of mucus that my body used to keep my lungs clear. I didn't do well in these kinds of conditions, and the physical strain had been intense. I downed Pedialyte like it was life itself, then I took a deep breath and remounted.

Down and down and down to the fire roads below. Three miles was all it was.

Three miles.

And three hours later, somehow I was on the other side of it. All of my skills came together that day. Enduro was very much Stacy's realm, whereas street was very much mine, so to have gotten the chance to do this with her made the whole trip.

Twenty-five miles an hour had never felt so fast, as we shot through a flowing stretch of woodsy single track to arrive at the truck. No sooner had we rolled Stacy's Freeride onto her hitch carrier did a forest service ranger come up to talk to us. They were closing the forests as of 5:00PM that day, he said. Despite the wide spread blaze and high temperatures, they had run into two people building campfires that day, and they had to shut everything down to save people from themselves. On a densely smoky, 90 degree day, I was almost flabbergasted. But I often remembered that the only thing more infinite than the universe itself would always be human stupidity.

With a shrug and a "thanks for letting us know," he tipped his hat and we drove back down the mountain.

On the way back to Lancaster, we stopped into a quirky café.

I ordered what would prove to be the worst burger I'd ever eaten, (which is saying something considering I'd had some sort of dog meat hamberguesas in the ruralist Latin America) and then I perused the menu for what really mattered.

"I'll take one sundae." I announced with pride.

"Would you like nuts?" The cashier asked.

"No." I shook my head. "I'll take sprinkles. Sprinkles are for winners."

The calm before the storm. As the trail got tougher and tougher, I kept thinking we'd finally found the worst of it. But OH how wrong I was. (Gold Mountain, California)

When we stopped for our first snack break, I finally felt like someone had cued me in on the joke. But after everything I'd been through already this summer, I was still game to try. (Gold Mountain, California)

Stacy went first to demonstrate the line. Which is good, because from a visual standpoint, looking at it from the edge, that mass of loose stones didn't offer any obvious route to ease the passage. (Gold Mountain, California)

Roads? Where we're going, we don't need roads. (Gold Mountain, California)

"So you like rocks? I have just the trail for you!" ~ Exceprt from conversations I regret having (Gold Mountain, California)

Being a big and heavy dual sport bike, Hollywood's KLX250 wasn't exactly suited to this kind of terrain either. But as the saying goes: A master painter can make art with any brush. (Gold Mountain, California)

Stacy was having a blast, introducing us to her favorite trail. I was just jealous that my hair never looks that fabulous after getting all sweaty in a helmet. (Gold Mountain, California)

After the unholy rock garden, the trail got tremendously easier, and resembled something more akin to what I wrestled in my early days in Colorado. (Gold Mountain, California)

The faces of three people who just survived the gnarliest thing I've ever seen... and who are definitely about to get some mother fucking sprinkles on their ice cream. (Big Bear, California)

Chapter 17

With all of the forests shut down, there wasn't much else we could do in California. I was bummed about it for a number of reasons. Since I started travelling and had gotten together with Hollywood, it had been incredibly rare that we spent any time in Los Angeles, so it was also incredibly rare that I had opportunities to see my friends. But with the forests shut down, we couldn't meet up to ride. And with the pandemic as it was, a majority of my friends weren't interested in spending time with someone who wasn't actively locked inside their home. So I felt at a bit of a loss as to how to proceed.

Hollywood's friends being heavily on the side of conservative politics tended to not care about COVID. My friends being heavily on the side of liberal politics tended to care in excess about COVID. And I just sat there feeling distraught and depressed that I was finally home after so many years of constant travel and, despite being healthy and fine, and despite all of my friends being healthy and fine, none of us were allowed to see each other. I'd never felt so lonely in a place where I knew and loved so many people.

But temporary politics weren't worth damaging my friendships permanently over, so I let them live their lives, and I lived mine with anyone who was willing to join me in the interim. There was still a constant veil of sadness that tainted every interaction I had, and being back in California was unfortunately making that worse instead of better, so we set up one more play date with Stacy and planned to head out until things improved.

Fortunately, while all of the forests were shut down, the deserts weren't, and Stacy knew a great spot in Johnson Valley.

We drove out to the middle of the desert on a warm, mid-90s day, and we unloaded on terrain that I'd not yet confronted in earnest.

Sand. So much sand. Everywhere we looked was loose and deep, threatening to swallow me whole in its soft and wobbly surface.

I wanted to get better in the sand, but even as I watched video after video on how to do it, every tip could just be summed up as "Go faster and don't be a bitch." Which is basically the most worthless and upsetting way you can give me advice. But there was no way to get comfortable enough to do that without practicing, so here we were and here I was.

The desert was packed with other riders, as it often is on any given weekend in the Golden State, and our pit area was filled with Stacy's usual dirt bike friends. She ran a group called Dirt Ladies, but her Dirt Ladies events were inclusive of husbands and boyfriends, too. Which I appreciated a lot, honestly. I've never been a big fan of the "girls only" thing. Don't get me wrong, I definitely can recognize that testosterone free events tend to have a different vibe, and I've had a lot of fun at charity track days where the men in attendance are only there to assist in the pits for the women riding on track. But, honestly, I find the events that exclude all men completely to be somewhat backwards and sexist in their own way. The idea is to create a safe space where women don't have to deal with the egos and opinions of men, and some women seem to love the segregation.

Being surrounded by other women and supporting other women is great and all, but I don't want or need a segregated space in order to do that, locked away from everyone else. I can love and build up my motorcycle sisters anywhere. If anything, I think it's more powerful to support each other among people who would challenge our worth, loud and open and proud.

Besides, being a girl who has always existed in male dominated spaces, from video games to comic books to software development to motorcycles, my friends have always been a mix of mostly guys and a few similarly minded girls, just because that's who I tend to encounter doing those hobbies. So I've never been uncomfortable with co-ed in any of my lifestyle choices, and I don't really feel the need to exclude people at something that's supposed to be fun.

But regardless, I really enjoyed the way she ran her Dirt Ladies events, with a big group of excited, badass women and the guys who are just as excited to share and support them in the lifestyle. It felt healthy and inclusive in the best ways possible.

But Johnson Valley was much less of an inclusive environment with its endless sand pits and nondescript landscape that was near impossible to visibly navigate. The distant rock piles all looked the same and the long rows of sand that cut between the desert shrubbery had no distinguishing marks to differentiate which slightly sloping path we might need to take.

This wouldn't have been a big deal if we hadn't taken off with a group of ladies who we found ourselves quickly separated from. They were looking to go far faster through the sand than I knew how to, and I'm very much a "ride your own ride" kind of person.

This was where I learned of another critical mistake I'd been making without even thinking about it. Having been following friends and GPS trail maps in places with clear, defined terrain so much lately, the concept of a big open sand box made it easy to get lost and have no idea how to get back. All of the rock mounds in the distance looked the same. So did all of the sand and shrubbery. I hadn't thought to mark camp with a beacon, so my cell phone map did zero good. At best, I could head towards the highway, where I knew I could approximately find my way back again, but navigating back on my own, when we'd made a number of just slightly curving turns that I couldn't retrace if I tried, was easier said than done.

Hollywood waited back with me along with a French couple who we had briefly met that morning. Chris and Sara had matching DR400s , though after struggling in the sand for a bit, Sara found herself wishing for something a little easier to pick back up. Hollywood was more than game to trade his 250 for her 400, and she was thrilled to have a bike she was more comfortable on. After some musical bikes, we all turned around together and started finding our way back.

Lost in the desert with a group of riders on appropriate and inappropriate bikes, I quickly found myself even more lost as Hollywood used all the horsepower of his borrowed DR400, and took off with a blaze of dust into the horizon. Sara and I were left behind, as both of us tried to figure out what direction was right.

I followed whatever vague sand roads looked maybe correct, fighting the bike as it flopped and wobbled through the deep, soft trails. My front wheel washed out in every which way, until we found ourselves in a very unfamiliar rock garden. The hills that I thought were camp were more of an impassible wall of stacked boulders, and try as we might to find the right way over the mound, nothing seemed to be correct. This certainly wasn't the way we came, but I couldn't say how far off that path we might be.

Hollywood found us as we circled to the left, then circled to the right, looking for the way through. It might have been more high stress if not for the fact that I was much more comfortable billy-goating over these rocks than I ever was in the sand. This detour felt a little bit like an oasis of manageable riding in the middle of a big, confusing mess.

Just when I started to feel that we would never find the way back, picking one wrong way after the other, out of water and out of options, someone in a UTV came ripping by. We waved them down to ask for directions.

The woman and her husband were happy to help. They shared some refreshments from the full sized cooler on the back of their rig (such luxury!) and then pointed us in the right direction.

Something I often find intimidating when in the desert like this, which is an issue I had my first time ever trying to ride a dirt bike on my own, is how easy it is to be out in the middle of nowhere, where no one will ever find you. You can get lost forever, even when someone else is right over the hill, because the vast, open nature of desert sand boxes is that everything is so open, you might never cross the same trail as someone else even in the overcrowded world of Southern California.

That's why I found myself pushing a flooded motorcycle back a whole mile of trail in a park as popular as Gorman OHV Park in Hungry Valley on a Saturday all those years ago. And why I determined that riding alone was a terrible idea on a dirt bike.

But luck was on our side this day, and these passersby were all we needed to get back on track. We'd missed the trail by about a thousand feet, it turned out.

As we approached our original tire tracks, lo and behold, we happened upon the rest of the group all on their way back. They had headed off to some other rock hills, and we caught them at exactly the right time. Maybe my luck isn't all bad after all.

They offered to lead the group back, and one of the other girls offered to trade me her lowered Husqvarna 300 two-stroke, just so I could see how difficult my little bike was making my life in terrain like this.

I reluctantly agreed, and she took off on my KLX. It wasn't long before everyone took off again, and I was on the wrong path again, now lost, alone, and on an unfamiliar bike.

That might have been more tragic if I this unfamiliar bike didn't glide over the sand like a balloon might loft through the sky. The suspension absorbed every rock and imperfection, transferring none of the forces to my spine. I could stand up, comfortably and easily. Power pulled me up hills, as though I was being beamed up by helpful aliens.

Perhaps there was a reason that everyone liked these KTM and Husqvarna two strokes, beyond insatiably drinking the orange Kool-Aid.

Perhaps.

So distracted by my sudden ability to ride over all obstacles without the pain of my actions having an equal reaction, I somehow ended up in someone else's camp spot. An old man sat outside his toy hauler with his dog, cooking some hot dogs on a grill, and watching me curiously, as I braaaped a few circles around this random rock face.

"Looking for someone?" He asked, as I came to a stop a few feet away.

"Did a bunch of girls on dirt bikes come through here?" I responded with defeat.

"Nope."

"Have you seen any other campers out here?"

"Nope."

My expression flattened. How far off was I?

I thanked him anyway and got back on the bike. Some more rocks and a small hill rested in the near distance. I had never been more grateful as I crested that hill, and the Dirt Ladies flag came into view.

I'm fairly certain I went faster in those last 100 yards than I had gone all day, as I raced back to the truck. I downed as much water as I could physically drink, and I collapsed into my camp chair.

The one good thing that I got out of this was, after all those miles, I was starting to feel a little more comfortable in the sand in general. I wasn't good at it by any stretch. And going faster didn't really seem to smooth things out as much as people said it would on the small bike. But all in all, I was better off than I was before.

It was only a matter of time before this boot camp took me to this kind of terrain, and I knew that it would be integral to learn to ride sand for my round the world trip. From the Baja to Morocco to Africa and South America, sliding around without having a mental and emotional breakdown was a skill I was finally perfecting. I wanted to fill this disappointing year of ruined life plans with something that was useful for the future, and this was becoming surprisingly satisfying and helpful as pre-round-the-world training.

I smiled silently to myself as I peeled of sweat-soaked gear under the blazing desert sun. I returned to the group, who was excitedly recounting each person's account of their ride, and I twisted open a cold bottle of water.

Together with strangers who were now friends, we spent the afternoon testing our balance through slow races and joking among ourselves.

It was a wonderful weekend. And the perfect build up for what was next.

The final graduation of all of my work that summer:

Moab, Utah.

The end of the day just meant the start of the shenanigans. We started with a circle race, where if you got passed, you were out, until there was only one person standing. (Cougar Butte, California)

Then we progressed to a slow race, where you had to move as slowly as possible, while maintaining enough balance that you don't have to put a foot down. (Cougar Butte, Calfornia)

A "Slow Race" probably doesn't sound like a roaring good time, but you might be surprised how difficult it is to keep your feet on the pegs without any momentum. (Cougar Butte, California)

The Dirt Ladies events drew quite a lot of girls who loved to rip dirt bikes. Fortunately, with such a large and varied group, there were riding buddies in your skill level for everyone. (Cougar Butte, California)

Everything kind of looks the same in the desert. I didn't know which stupid patch of sand was going to take me home, and which was going to take me to more stupid patches of sand. (Cougar Butte, California)

I'm pretty sure this picture went something like:
"Dude. We're lost."
"No, we're fine."
"No, dude, we're definitely lost."
"No. We're. Fine." Cue going in panicked circles. (Cougar Butte, California)

It was a great weekend with a great group of ladies (And lady support crew) that I'm stoked to now call friends! Looking forward to riding with them again in the future! (Cougar Butte, California)

Chapter 18

I'd been to Moab once before. Though it was limited to the roads and hiking trails of Arches National Park, as I was on my street bike on my first 49 state tour. I accidentally showed up on Memorial Day weekend, and the red rock cliffs were so packed, I ended up camping in a dirt parking lot at the side of the road, exposed to the wind, on ground too physically hard to stake. I left without exploring much, so while it was often touted as an off road paradise, I hadn't the vaguest concept of what the world looked like once your tires left blacktop.

With a couple bucket list destinations in Utah that I had somehow still never hit, we decided to make a big trip of it. We broke up the drive through southern Utah over several days, taking the time to explore some of the National Parks along the way. Zion may as well have been closed to the public, allowing only a handful of permits per day for exploring the park, so we simply drove through that one without stopping. Fortunately, that was the one spot I had been to and hiked a good bit already. It remains my favorite National Park.

Bryce Canyon I had never been to, however, so we spent a day hiking around the most popular and scenic features of the park. The staggering stone columns, painted in the vibrant reds of the iron rich dirt of southern Utah, and split by bright green rivers and plants, made for a feast for the eyes. I still think this portion of the world is one of the most uniquely beautiful places I've ever had the good fortune to visit.

Escalante, Utah's "giant staircase," was the next stop. We hiked into deep slot canyons and admired sandstone columns that had been twisted and sculpted by erosion. Though the road into Escalante may have been the worst road I've ever had the displeasure to follow for 80 miles. It wasn't rutted, nor were there rocks, but the heavy RV traffic had created relentless washboards, which shook our truck to pieces for the entirety of the five hours in and five hours out.

It didn't help that we ended up with a flat tire about 75 miles in from running over a piece of sharp shale. I could hear the hissing out the window, every bump and rotation of the tire. Fortunately, a plug and a large screw was enough to nurse the truck to a roadside tire repair shop in the nearby town of Hanksville. In a Mexico-like fashion, the tire guy rolled our damaged wheel into a plywood shack, roughly built in a wide and uneven dirt parking lot. He dismounted and patched the tire from the inside, then had the wheel back to us within about fifteen minutes for a meager $20. That's ten times the price of a tire patch at a Mexican llantera, but that was the best I could ask for on this side of the border.

We continued our trek through Capital Reef National Park, stopping here and there to admire the petroglyphs from peoples long past. Capital Reef is one of those parks that I've never really heard anyone talk about, but the way the stones twist and stack and erode upon themselves is truly a vision worthy of its national park status. Definitely an underrated place.

An entire week of playing the tourist later, we at long last arrived in Moab itself. We sat in a line of traffic several miles long, as every single jobless person who had recently bought themselves a bunch of off road toys with their unemployment money lined up to take over the hills.

It was… not quite what I expected. Especially since I had been led to believe this was the off season. And I'll admit that as we dwindled down our savings more and more each week, I was a touch jealous of all these brand new campers and 30+ thousand dollar side-by-sides that I couldn't afford. The fact that the abundance of people had also driven up the price of hotels didn't help either, though we had intended to camp regardless.

We hauled ourselves up the hill to Porcupine Rim Campground, a solid 20 miles off a long dirt road that climbed into the cliffs that overlooked the town. Here, we were meeting some old friends. We sat on the ledge, kicking our feet side by side, while we watched the sun set over the deep canyon floor below us. The reddest reds and the pinkest pinks blanketed the landscape. Vague trails could be discerned between desert trees and the Colorado River. Beautiful. A beauty we would soon conquer under our two wheels.

I pitched the tent while Hollywood built us a campfire, and in quiet solitude, we enjoyed the black sky and bright full moon that illuminated those pink and purple slick rocks of Moab. These quiet nights in the wilderness, just the two of us, were some of my favorite nights of all. We talked into the late hours, then snuggled in our tent until the sun, peeking through the thin walls of our tent, woke us up.

Carolanne and Dennis showed up the following day to ride with us. For some reason, Dennis didn't seem terribly thrilled to be there, but Carolanne was raring to go. Maybe the prospect of riding with some slow beginners wasn't that exciting for a more advanced rider, or maybe this just wasn't his kind of place, but I didn't know enough about Moab to guess why he was less than enthused.

Fortunately, Carolanne was a fireball of energy, which my natural empathetic tendencies quickly melded with. The last time she had been in Moab, she rented a dirt bike. But being brand new to two wheels had made the terrain difficult and daunting. Now that she had been practicing all summer, she was exciting to redo some of the places that previously held her up. Conquering old challenges with new ease is one of my favorite things about riding, so I was more than game to let her lead the way.

Hurrah Pass was our first destination. It's the kind of wide dirt road that's got just enough rocks and small step ups and deep sand to be interesting and fun, but not so much that it's challenging or scary. After our time in California and Southern Colorado, this was welcome comfort. Something easy. Something not death defying. Something that didn't require extra hydration to compensate for tears. I nearly forgot that this was possible while also riding a dirt bike. I don't know if I've ever gotten to ride a trail that was fun in an enjoyable way instead of in a bad joke with malicious intent kind of way. What a pure and simple joy this was. The views were quintessential Moab, from the breathtaking red rock canyons, to the hoodoo caves and catacombs.

There was nothing overly noteworthy about the ride itself, other than maybe the deep and steep sand hill that my California training somehow got me up without incident. Being only a short exclamation point of an otherwise manageable ride, I had a lot of fun engaging my mind and riding muscles for that short stretch, then turning my brain back off and bee-bopping along once I was done.

Double points when Dennis stalled his bike in the sand, which could only be started via bump start. Watching Hollywood and Dennis push the bike while their boots sunk into the ground with every step, trying their darndest to get the KTM to fire up again was popcorn worthy.

Otherwise, Hollywood and Dennis were buzzing by me through the turns with their legs out like they were Ricky Brabec, and Carolanne and I were pushing each other along with our laughter. The gorgeous catacomb cavern at the end of the ride let our inner children climb around the rocks like they were a jungle gym, and Carolanne made us all lunch with some snack mix, tortillas and packaged tuna. Good snacks are perks of travelling with someone who's a mom.

I was loving Moab as we turned back and got to view the canyons again, now from the other angle. Even as my tires dug into the deep sand slopes, and a bad line choice had my ambition (and ground clearance) outweighing my talent on a rocky step down, I was still having fun. I was also having bruises, but happy little bruises. It made for an inspiring and relaxing first day of riding. This had been a great choice.

Day two, we opted to explore the La Sal Mountains just outside our camp. Hurrah Pass had required we truck our bikes over and unload and reload, since most of us weren't riding street legal dirt bikes, but this one we could ride to directly from our base camp. There's something inherently pleasant about being able to just throw on your gear and go, without the theatrics of truck ramps and tie downs.

Today, we aimed for Kokopelli trail.

One (or eight) wrong turns took us to an uncertain shortcut through some ranch land. Autumn leaves covered the dirt in thick patches of brown, orange, and yellow. My tires followed the narrow rails of raised dirt in between deep ruts until we came upon the first barbed wire fence.

We looked at each other, thinking we had taken a wrong turn yet again, when Hollywood unceremoniously dismounted, unhooked a tree branch wrapped in barbed wire, and dragged open the gateway.

Carolanne and Dennis both looked between each other uncomfortably.

"It's public land. We just have to close the gate behind us." He shrugged.

I apologized to them both with a nervous laugh, but pulled back on my helmet just the same. "This is basically every day when you ride in Montana."

I was the first through the gate, and the first to drive my wheels straight into a stray cow pie. This is also basically every day when you ride in Montana, I thought to myself.

The bovine poop was plentiful on this connecting route, and the mud was slick and wet. We followed a mountainside for a few miles, pushing through the overgrown bushes, now colored by those delightful bright reds and yellows of the season. A bush exploded against my chest in autumn confetti, speckling the mountain side in celebration. The ruts were challenging but manageable, and the cow ravaged pits weren't exactly a comforting ride, but I was so enamored with the world we were in, I didn't want it to end. I couldn't imagine any way that Kokopelli could top the detours we took to get there, but I was certainly willing to let it try.

Another barbed wire gate marked the end of the shortcut, and then we at long last arrived at our destination. This trail seemed to be most popular with the abundance of mountain bikers who barreled by on pedal bikes that far exceeded the value of my motorbike. We had to choose careful lines down the deep ruts and ledged slick rock, while also picking careful lines to dodge these rolling obstacles.

I rolled on ahead, oblivious to my companions, until I arrived at the bottom, alone and victorious. I was back on the fire road to Porcupine Rim Campground, and the familiarity squashed any potential anxiety of being lost.

Seeing a rare opportunity for riding photos, I settled in to play photographer, while everyone else did whatever they were doing that was taking so long. One by one, they rolled down the last ledge. Dennis did a wheelie. Hollywood Launched himself off the highest step. The stoke was high.

High enough to try one more ride that day. And what better ride than the Porcupine Rim Trail itself?

Porcupine Rim the trail, it turns out, is the first real Moab trail to cross our paths. These fun and colorful and easy routes that we had been doing were outliers in the jagged mess that was true Moab. Unlike the Porcupine Rim Campground that inspires zen and good feelings, the associated trail inspires carnage and self-loathing. And this was supposed to be one of the easier Jeep trails in the area! I'd learn more about the rest in the coming week.

This whole ride became a violent mess of rock steps, more suited to stable, high clearance Rubicons than any sort of gravity adverse motorcycle. There were no lines of relief, and no smooth outer edges to help dodge the extremity of the steps. It was pushing and pulling and dragging my bike, while praying to the gods that my bike could roll down other steps without bottoming and throwing me over the ledge.

Honestly, it wasn't fun at all. It was an exercise in white knuckle survival and physically lifting my bike over obstacles like it was the world's most worthless paperweight. By Carolanne's third crash, one almost tipping her bike off the cliff side, we opted to turn around. I was thankful that Hollywood was nearby enough to help her heave the bike back onto the mountain before the trail ruined an otherwise brilliant weekend.

I'd say I was proud to be keeping my own bike upright, but it was only thanks to it being short and walkable. At 5'6" with a 30" inseam, I won't say I have long legs, but they were just long enough to get good footing on the 125 even when it was cocked between a ledge and an incline. Still, this ride was all work and no play, and I was beginning to doubt that the reward at the end was going to be worth the torture and dwindling daylight we would risk to get there. We were already camped at the other side of this trail after all, so if we really wanted to see the epic view, well, we could walk a few steps from bed.

Still, the day was epic, even with an early turn around. You have to know when to call it sometimes, and let me tell you, the incredible steaks and asparagus that Carolanne whipped up at camp that night were well worth calling it for.

This was our last night with Coralanne and Dennis before they returned home to Silverthorne, and it was a bittersweet goodbye. I really loved riding with Carolanne. She was the only person who I had ridden with all summer who was learning along with me, conquering obstacles for the first time with me, and willing to make rational decisions that didn't involve yelling "send it!" with me. I liked riding with other people, too, but with her, there was always a sense of comradery and mutual assured protection. Plus, she brought with her so much cheer and enthusiasm, that even my most depressed moments were often suppressed and forgotten.

Between Stacy and Carolanne, it was nice to feel empowered riding with others again instead of feeling like the weak link. Goodbyes were inevitable, but the confidence I gained would stay with me. Which was good, because it was bound to get a lot more challenging over the next couple days.

*Deep reds, sculpted canyons, and towering plateaus—
Hurrah Pass was everything you imagine when someone
says Southern Utah. (Moab, Utah)*

*The Catacombs on the other side of Hurrah Pass meant we
had a full day of exploring on bikes and a full day of
exploring like Indiana Jones. Moab is neat! (Moab, Utah)*

Even Hollywood is capable of deep pondering at times. Either that, or he's thinking about how good a cold beer is going to taste when we get back. (Moab, Utah)

There is nothing—and I mean nothing—more soothing than an icy cold dip of a sore and battered body after a long day of riding. (Moab, Utah)

Our shortcut to Kokopelli Trail was a highlight of the day, with enough challenge to be interesting, enough simplicity to be fun, and enough fall colors to be beautiful. (Moab, Utah)

You know it's getting good when we start casting "I don't know about this" glances at each other. (Moab, Utah)

After we both struggled and flailed on the Porcupine Rim Trail for a while, Carolanne nearly losing her bike over the edge seemed like as good a time to call it as any. (Moab, Utah)

While Hurrah pass taunted us with a few rocks sticking out of the dirt, Porcupine Rim Trail just straight up laughed at us. (Moab, Utah)

Chapter 19

With Carolanne and Dennis heading home, we loaded up our camping gear and headed down into town to meet up with Chris. Chris was more of a hotel guy than a roughing it guy, so generally when we rode together, he preferred for us to be parked together in the same establishment.

Though it was a wonder that we were able to get a spot at all, as the entire town was packed to the brim. Hundreds, if not thousands, of vehicles lined the streets of downtown Moab, leaving little room for even our modest size truck and motorcycles, and the only room available for less than $150 a night was tucked away from the rest of the hotel with the cleaning ladies.

I would complain, but Chris had agreed to help split the bill. Marshal had come down as well, and with no other prospects, he offered to split the room and bill, too, so it was almost affordable. I was still choking up dust from our four days of camping anyways, breathing in a never clearing mist of fine red particles from the endless parade of side-by-sides, so a clean room was a welcome change.

After my time at Gold Mountain, I felt ready to be challenged by Moab's "hard stuff," and Chris was generally pretty good at finding that kind of terrain. He was also generally patient and encouraging enough to let me sort my way through it.

If it had just been me, Hollywood, Chris, and Marshal, I think this week would have been a fantastic development of my desert skills.

But it wasn't.

Unbeknownst to the rest of us—or if Hollywood knew, he chose not to tell me—Chris had invited six of his most badass riding friends, who were all Moab regulars. They all had the most tricked out dirt bikes money could buy. They all had ridden every trail in Moab, from the most challenging to the most simple, many times, and I didn't know a single one of them.

Apparently this Moab trip was an annual thing for all of them, and they already had a whole itinerary of wild riding in mind. What was sold to me as "let me show you around Moab" quickly turned into "Good luck tagging along on our gnar trip," and I found myself overwhelmed right out the gate.

I'm not going to say that I have performance anxiety, but I'm definitely one of those people who doesn't even like typing an email if there's someone standing over my shoulder watching me. Knowing I was the least advanced rider among a group of six guys who I didn't know made it difficult for me to ever feel comfortable. They all seemed nice enough in our very brief meeting the night before, so I hoped these worries would be unfounded. The first day of riding together would answer that.

My fears were very soon realized when a rushed morning and having to miss breakfast had me out of sorts before the ride even started. I'm very much a breakfast person. I've always been a breakfast person. And I suspect that I will always be a breakfast person. But when even the gas station was completely out of all food and snacks due to the unusually high tourist traffic, and when all of the other guys are so antsy to get moving that waiting for restaurants to open wasn't an option, it's a recipe for a very disoriented Tiff.

I tried to collect myself and swallow my stomach grumbles as we unloaded and geared up at the base of Seven Mile Rim. Chris and his friends were all on dual sport bikes, so they geared up in the hotel as soon as they woke up, then waited around at the trail head for Hollywood and I to get ready. Hollywood was being irritable, blaming me for every second we held them up because of my non-plated bike, only adding to my self-consciousness, and I was overwhelmed by the stress of it all before the day's ride even started. Instantly I was the odd one out in this group of badasses and hardcore riders, and intentional or not, everyone was making sure that I was aware of this.

The only calm I felt that morning was the briefest moment, as I listened to the sound of my little 8 horsepower engine fire up on the first kick. At least my bike was on my side.

Now, if Porcupine Rim was a giant's staircase, Seven Mile Rim was the cliff the giant got pushed off of in the first place. It was here that I came to learn the true extent of "Jeep Trails" that is Moab.

Every open stretch was deep sand, where there was no hope that I might keep up to the fleet of ultra-light two strokes. And every hard packed section was a series of tall rock shelves. I managed a few lines. Botched a few others. At one point, I wedged myself into a crevasse, one half of my bike atop the shelf, the other below, and a wall in the way to prevent forward momentum. I was essentially dead squatting the weight of my KLX125 to surmount every obstacle, then wrestling to stay upright through deep sand on every section that was supposed to act as relief.

The heat and hunger started to get to me, and it seemed to be getting to Hollywood, too. At one point Hollywood crashed into Chris while trying to surmount a blind step up, not realizing Chris was still atop it. At other points, I was pretending to not be miserable as I nursed my increasing dehydration with the always inadequate number of water bottles we brought along.

From the very beginning, it was one of those days where I wasn't in the right headspace to be riding in the first place. Let alone riding gnarly stuff. About 10 miles in, when I arrived at the rest spot a solid 15 minutes behind the rest of the guys, I'd had enough. Everyone else was zipping along, hanging out, and brainstorming what heart stopping obstacle they were going to conquer next, and I was back to feeling like a burden who was holding everyone back.

I resented my inability. I was back to square one, rattled and unhappy and hating dirt bikes again. This should have been fun. But being the one weak link among a big group of eager and advanced riders who I didn't know at all was my personal hell. I found myself draining of confidence through a one-way valve, while a parade of gnomes dumped in buckets of doubt in its place. There was nothing in that terrain that I couldn't do other than keep up, but that was enough for my over critical self-admonishment to rear its ugly head.

When we at last caught up with the group, who was sitting at a wide, flat, slick rock rest area, Hollywood and I opted to split off from the rest of them to explore easier terrain. Chris had his doubts that I could handle the big obstacles, and he expressed as such, mentioning spots with friendly names like Wipeout Hill and Determination Towers, and without anyone's vote of confidence, I was better off tapping out. The big group headed out, and we took to the desert alone, looking for a loop that supposedly would return us to the parking lot.

Like much of my life, neither of us had any clue as to where we were going. Everything looked the same, between long sand roads and rocky rocks. We had no map and there wasn't any clear signage. Much like we had done in Johnson Valley, we ended up making a series of wrong turns that only lead us deeper and deeper into the vast open nothingness of the red desert. Worse yet, when we did find the looping trail, it had been closed to motorized traffic, and we had to do our best to backtrack. The scenery was gorgeous, but not enough to soften my stress. We ran out of water, we strayed way off path in the hardest terrain I'd ever suffered through, and by the time we found the truck again, I was beat and over it and just wanted to cry.

The lot was empty. Everyone else had finished their rides and long since returned to comfort and food. Hollywood decided to ride back to the hotel on his bike, so he could better integrate into the group. I sat alone in the truck, staring at nothing, shaking, upset, and terrified of what this week was going to look like.

When riding the street—particularly in the case of canyons and the like—I'm extremely picky about who I ride with, and there are a lot of reasons for that. Early in my riding career, I was desperate to make friends. I was 21 years old, didn't know anyone who rode motorcycles, and I had been on my own out in the wild for months, so a group ride posted on a local motorcycle forum was my chance to meet some people. Cool guys in full leather body suits, who talked about the stickiest tires and the steepest lean angles and the fastest lap times in the canyons filled the Del Taco parking lot in Azusa, California as we prepared to tear through the "mad twisties" of Glendora Mountain Road. The group as a whole was far more advanced than I was. I didn't know their riding styles or what was expected of me. I had no idea how any of this worked. I'd ridden canyons alone, but alone, there's no pressure to perform or keep up.

So I just started up my bike and came along for the ride.

This group of fourteen or so riders tore down the street with a vengeance, and I did my best to fit in, speeding up to stay with the group. As the road got tight and twisty, it was a full on battle to keep pace. I hadn't been to the track yet—this was actually the event that convinced me to start doing track days—but I was doing my best to mimic the riders around me so I could keep up.

Long story short, I ate shit trying to over correct and lean harder into a decreasing radius turn at speed.

One or two riders stopped to make sure I was okay. The rest continued down the mountain. And I stared at the cliff that was just inches from swallowing my bike whole.

It was my first lesson that, in this extremely dangerous sport, you have to ride your own ride, but also that you had to be able to trust the riders you're riding with. A group that doesn't support each other isn't any group worth riding with, and the weakest link is as important as the strongest.

Yes, as I got older and more mature, I learned to also say "to hell with those idiots" and I no longer gave in to peer pressure, but I also had no desire to ride with people who even brought peer pressure to the table. If someone has no sense of self-preservation or discipline on a bike, I don't particularly want to be around them even if I'm in no risk myself.

I've had to disown friends who were incredibly unsafe riders, not wanting to have to be there when they inevitably maimed themselves riding like idiots on the road (and they always did eventually). Being able to trust your riding companion is everything, both when things go wrong and when things are going right, and the wrong riding buddy can completely ruin a trip. If I didn't know or trust that a rider wouldn't, say, start doing wheelies in traffic and crash into a parked car, or if they were the type of hot head to make me feel bad for not letting them provoke me into riding over my head, or even if we just straight up weren't compatible as riders in terms of distance, comfort standards, and frequency (or infrequency) of stopping, I didn't ride with them.

Does that make me a snob?

Probably.

But am I sorry about this?

Absolutely-fucking-not.

On the street, this was a well-established rule that no one ever argued with me over. While I still have an excess of compassion and empathy to my detriment in many places in my life (that I very much need to work on), road riding was not one of those places. Dirt riding, however, I was still coming to understand. And very quickly I was learning that those boundaries needed to exist here, too.

I arrived at the hotel, where everyone else was already sitting in a circle, enjoying an adult beverage or two, and I tried to better get to know the group. I hadn't even gotten to explain my side before I was being bombarded with unsolicited advice. Things like "go faster in the sand and it'll be easier" and tips on the most basic aspects of bike control. In the group's eyes, I was practically a first time rider, where they still had to teach me what a clutch was. I hadn't performed well enough to defend myself, and I knew it.

My spirits sank lower still.

The following day was a chance at a better second impression. I pulled the cover over my head as Marshal stomped around the hotel room before the sun rose, so he could get in enough riding before the riding started, then I snatched some remaining granola bars from the hotel lobby before the overbooked guest list could completely deplete the supply.

This day, the goal was a nearby trail called Slick Rock. While the name sounded daunting and void of traction, the slick misnomer came from old Mormon settlers who found the surface to be incredibly slippery when crossing by horse. On a motorcycle, however—or with any modern vehicle with modern sticky tires—the sand paper like surface on the visually smooth and rounded stone was actually *incredibly* grippy.

Even having been told this, and doing the mental gymnastics required to kind of believe it, no one had warned me how completely vertical these ascents and descents would be. I thought I had finally mastered going downhill, but not until I was staring straight down at the steepest grades I'd ever encountered, on hills I wouldn't even be able to hike down without sliding on my butt (or climb back up without using my hands for support) did I realize that my anxiety hadn't mastered shit.

A mile of near vertical drops and inclines that twisted over the massive boulders, with drop offs on either side, I was in over my head, and my survival instincts made sure I knew it. The trail was overflowing with mountain bikers and motor bikers, to the point that the more challenging obstacles had waiting queues, where we'd line up and wait our turn. The pressure from strangers who would yell and complain if you took too long didn't help. I was shaken from day one with Chris and his crew, and I just couldn't seem to recover.

My mind didn't trust the grip no matter how good it was in reality. I was miserable, I was struggling, and the big group of extremely advanced dudes all around me, hooting and hollering about how fun and easy it all was, made me feel like utter garbage. It wasn't just hard, it was hard and emotionally debilitating and depressing.

We hadn't even made it to the start of the lollipop shaped loop, when a talk with Hollywood and Chris made it clear I just needed to give up. I let everyone else go on without me, and I took a break under the shade of a stone overhang to contemplate my life choices.

This wasn't how it was supposed to be. I'd been looking forward to this Moab trip since we first discussed spending the summer on dirt bikes. And now here I was, not being able to enjoy any of it, not just feeling left out, but feeling like I *deserved* to be left out. What good was I with my fear? No one else had fear. Even Marshal, who was a newer rider, never registered the slightest hint of self-doubt. It was only me. I was the only one who couldn't do it. And every day where that was shoved in my face, every high five that I couldn't share, just left me silently sobbing. If I had known I was just going to be the annoying little sister tagging along on the extreme boy's trip, I wouldn't have come at all.

As I rested under the shade, a group of guys in a side-by-side came by. They stopped to make sure I wasn't hurt. I assured them that I was simply a pussy.

"Well, your sense of humor sounds like it's still intact." The men laughed, before promptly offering me a half frozen bottle of water. Heaven on a hot day like this. They stopped to chat for a bit, letting me vent with welcoming smiles. The man in the driver's seat gave me a pat on the shoulder.

"You're out here on a motorcycle," he said. "There's nothing pussy about you."

Small, silly, and baselessly optimistic as those words may have been, my heart felt a little lighter after hearing them. It helped to be reminded of that sometimes. Even if by my standards, I was still the worst rider there was, every now and again, taking a step back to stop comparing myself to others so much and acknowledge what I *am* accomplishing, is more important than I can express in words. Being your own worst critic is the greatest curse of all passionate hobbyists.

They motored off, and I returned to my perch and watched the mountain bikers rolling by. Some could hop and roll over every obstacle, no matter how extreme, while many of them would get off their bikes completely, traversing the trails I couldn't by simply carrying or walking their bikes up or down the worst features. I envied the lightweight vehicles that gave them that option. A less advanced mountain biker wouldn't have to sit here, alone and friendless, unable to advance. They were allowed to choose their level of adventure, and still come home feeling like a winner.

A guide in a brand new Rubicon, taking a troop of tourists up a completely straight stone face came by. I watched in awe as the four wheel drive Jeep basically deadlifted itself from a total stop, completely vertical, straight up and over the wall. Incredible. I couldn't even believe a vehicle was capable of that without rolling backwards. The engineering of a well-built Jeep is far beyond anything I've ever seen. I had a new respect for the term "Jeep Trails."

While the tourists gawked at the canyon below, the guide approached me to make sure I was okay. I guess I must have looked pretty pathetic, sitting in the shade with a few bottles of water next to my bike. He offered me his number in case my friends didn't come back, and I needed help getting out. I thanked him, while still feeling a little pathetic. He told me how he used to ride a 250, himself, and he continued to gush about how much he loved my little bike. He made a special effort to let me know how impressed he was that I had made it this far at all.

That made me feel a little better, too. My tiny wheels and drum brakes didn't do me many favors compared to a lightweight two stroke with eighteen inches of ground clearance, and disc brakes that could stop on a dime. Not that I was confident enough to handle one of those tall bikes, so the superior equipment wouldn't have done me any better, but it was still a small bit of ego boost to remember I was using the worst equipment of everyone. And right now, I needed any boost I could get.

Chatting with friendly passersby started to make me feel better and more confident. So much so that I considered hopping back on my bike and trying to find the rest of the group. I built myself up in my head for a few moments and started putting on my helmet. Then I heard the sound of eight buzzing engines coming over the hill.

All eight riders came rolling down, one at a time, standing on their pegs, and picking the extra hard lines, where they launched themselves a few feet through the air, before skidding to a stop on the other side of the clearing. No one even acknowledged I was there, including Hollywood. I walked over to the group who was excited and full of adrenaline, having conversations I couldn't be included in. That resolve I'd been building up disappeared. My mood dropped right back to being the burdensome little sister who was ruining everyone else's awesome trip. Why did I come here again?

It was my fault I felt that way, I know. But I had come here thinking I'd be doing a fun and challenging ride with my friends, and they had come thinking they were ripping it up with their hardcore buddies, and there was no reason we should have been on the same ride. Alone with a group, I followed behind them with my tail between my legs, too depressed to even notice I was conquering these steep wild trails that had challenged me on the way in unconsciously.

Back at the hotel, it was more beginner advice, still barely a notch above "the throttle is on the right." I didn't know any of these guys well enough to have a non-motorcycle related conversation with any of them, so I just nodded along politely, trying to steal back some level of street cred with my road-based accomplishments and trying to explain how much I'd developed this summer versus the demons I still battled in the dirt, but it fell on deaf ears.

It's a funny thing as someone with anxiety, when you try to explain what it feels like to people who have never struggled with a real, visceral, internalized fear. Genuine empathy isn't as common a trait as I'd hope, so to explain having the ability to vividly imagine every worst possible scenario—every potential injury that might befall me when I messed up in any of the thousand ways that were playing in my head like I was watching a violent movie—and to have to cast aside those images, covering my ears and yelling "La La La" before EVERY. SINGLE. OBSTACLE I faced is a concept so far out of a non-anxious person's imagination that it was like speaking an alien language.

My over active imagination could picture even the most unlikely scenarios, while the group around me knew how to ignore that as bizarre and unlikely. At best, one of the other riders tried to relate to me by saying he once met a girl who had a panic attack once, so he kind of got it. That was about the time I gave up.

I wish I could have just stopped being scared—that I could have kept up with everyone and been confident and capable of ignoring high risk scenarios, but that took time that I hadn't been allotted. One day, I might have their easy confidence, but it would likely be years of baby steps instead of a few seconds of cliff jumping.

But as unhappy as I had become over these two bad rides, I knew I only had to grin and bear these struggles for just one more day.

The last day of riding we had planned was still up in the air. They talked about White Rim Trail, which they knew my bike was neither legal for nor had the fuel range to finish. Being the weak link and odd one out was the theme of that week, so it would have been par for the course if we had done it anyway.

I contemplated assuring everyone that I was okay with not riding at all. It was clear that I wasn't really a part of this trip in anyone's mind, and I felt outnumbered and unwelcome. I was miffed by my own inadequacy, and tired of trying to find impossible lines that my tiny wheels could handle on high clearance trails. At this point, to have any opinion at all was like being a stick in the mud who had been broken in half so many times, no one noticed they were stepping on it.

Watching me fake a smile and wish everyone well as they talked about riding something with an inviting name like "Poison Spider," it was finally Hollywood who decided I deserved some mercy that day.

"Why don't we just do Hurrah Pass today?" he suggested.

Chris was reluctant, knowing the rest of the guys would likely be bored on such an easy trail, since they were all there for the hardcore gnar.

I was intrigued though. One of those rare chances to repeat a trail sounded good. The last time that had happened, I had found myself with more comfort and speed than ever. I could use something that would improve my skill instead of spit on it right now.

Feeling excited for the first time in days, the end decision was that Hollywood, Marshal, and I would ride Hurrah Pass, Chris and his friends would go ride whatever death defying rock mountain they so fancied, and we'd simply regroup when we got back.

When we unloaded in the dirt parking lot, Hollywood waited for Marshal to show up. And I went on ahead alone. It was an easy trail with nothing to worry about, and it would give both of them a chance to stretch their legs catching up with me.

Much to my delight, with twice the speed and comfort of the first outing, I was flowing through the turns, picking good lines around the steps, and laughing in my helmet as my tires wriggled through the sand traps. I did still know how to laugh. I was starting to forget.

At a fork in the road, Hollywood and Marshal still out of sight, I stopped to talk to a mountain bike guide who was similarly waiting for his group. He had dread locks, a winning smile, and a KTM 500EXC at home that he often rode when he wasn't leading tourists around the red dust. He gave me tips about some local single track that he thought I might enjoy, and I felt a little more empowered and welcome in this land.

When Hollywood and Marshal caught up, we continued the rest of the way to the catacombs. The rocky caves were the perfect spot for a picnic, and we sat around enjoying trail snacks and our echoing voices, with all of us in good spirits.

When we got back to the hotel that day, I finally felt good. Like I had shrugged off the weights on my shoulders, shoved my self-loathing in a burn barrel, and could at long last breathe again. Even Marshal had enjoyed the speed and only moderate challenge of an easier trail. It was something different. We loaded up our bikes in the parking lot, everyone beaming and feeling refreshed, when Chris and the others returned from their ride.

Much to my surprise, they had also decided to do Hurrah Pass that day, and by oddly timed coincidence, we had just missed running into them when we turned off into the catacombs. They had, instead, ridden to a spot known as Chicken Corners, most famous for the filming of Thelma and Louise. Somehow we managed to time it so we both arrived at the hotel nearly at the same time while also missing each other completely.

At dinner, as we all debriefed that night, the guys were all in high spirits, having actually enjoyed getting to do such a fast flowing and manageable trail through Moab's intense beauty. Actually having the time to admire the scenery and flow around the corners was fun even for advanced riders, it turned out. I wish we could have started with this, so I could have gotten to know these people under positive circumstances, but I was willing to settle for simply ending the week on a high note instead of a low one.

As I reflected on the week over fine Indian food, finally getting to partake in the laughs instead of feeling like the butt of every disappointed joke, I felt good.

I've come a long way since we started this whole dirt bike adventure back in May. I'm still not the best rider, and I learned this week that my fear threshold certainly still exists no matter what kind of crazy obstacles I've somehow successfully ridden, but to compare my ability now to the girl who just about cried when she rode down a hill with, like, 8 rocks, is a transformation I didn't think was possible back when I was convinced dirt bikes would simply never be my thing.

I'm still not proud of how the week went. I was mad at myself for not being good enough. But I was comparing myself to a group of men who have been riding for a lifetime, on the best equipment with the best training, and that wasn't fair to anyone.

I had a long way to go, but don't we always when it comes to riding a motorcycle?

Riding my KLX125, with its tiny wheels, was a constant challenge in a place like Moab, where the slick rock shelves are often dramatic stairs and jagged pit falls. It took some creative lines to get myself around the worst obstacles. (Moab, Utah)

There are few things more stressful than being lost in the desert and knowing you're drinking your last bottle of water. (Moab, Utah)

A rare moment where we were all together. Ironically just minutes before we all split up. (Moab, Utah)

Slick Rock was crowded with both riders and mountain bikes. But for the first time ever, in the face of inclines, I was actually more jealous of the mountain bikers. (Moab, Utah)

Not sure if a trail or a wall. (Moab, Utah)

While everyone needs a little help sometimes, having to ask for it multiple times in a single trail wasn't exactly fun for my pride or my confidence. Which was such a shame after such an otherwise inspiring summer. (Moab, Utah)

While I don't mind not being the best or the fastest rider, being completely outclassed amongst a bunch of hardcore dirt bikers, with no one who wanted to have to ride with me, wrecked my excitement and morale. (Moab, Utah)

Chapter 20

Once everyone went their separate ways in Moab, Hollywood and I left without much of a plan. That was the last major destination we had on the list of must-ride places, and with winter fast approaching, the high mountain passes were beginning to lose their appeal. The first snow had already started to hit Colorado as we neared the end of October, and I wasn't looking to stud my tires again.

While I'd done that before when we lived in Montana, so mentally far gone in the 6+ month long winter of Northern Whitefish that even the most absurd ideas started to seem reasonable, carving up frozen lakes in a blizzard while -17°F ambient temperatures threatened to take your soul every time you slowed down, wasn't a level of desperation I'd ever like to revisit.

No, instead we started talking about riding south. We turned our noses towards Southern California again, stopping briefly at a place called Swing Arm City along the way.

The OHV park just outside Hanksville, Utah was strikingly unique, and with a name as cool as Swing Arm City, I couldn't resist. The park consisted of massive slopes on a dark gray dried lake bed that felt more like riding on the moon than on anything I'd expect in Southern Utah. Deep Ravines in the dark, cracked ground created circuits of narrow, single track canyons, which you could easily get lost in. And the steep natural ramps offered both death defying jumps into oblivion or heart skipping spine riding along the pointed crest of high cliffs.

None of this was particularly suited to either the 125 *or* the 250, but it was fun to spend an hour or two ripping through crumbling black earth that broke under the grip of our tire knobs.

On a Thursday afternoon, we had the place to ourselves, but high winds made it an unappealing place to camp. With a quick in and out, we were back on the road. Hollywood took the wheel, along with copious amounts of caffeine, planning to pound out the eighteen hour drive in one hit. I watched the country pass behind us under the setting sun, until only the light of the moon was left to illuminate the rounded spires and soft pink monoliths.

It should have felt like the end of a trip. Melancholy, confusing. But... I still felt like my trip had never really started. This summer of riding the back country wasn't the round the world trip of my dreams, and try as I might to convince myself I was equally happy with it—certainly it was helpful to my goals, and I accomplished a lot on a personal level—I couldn't shake that disappointment.

I had a goal, and it was far more complex and lofty than just fooling around in the mountains. Riding the back country was missing the exotic flair, the cultural awakenings, the new friends, the new enemies, the language barriers, and the uncertainty. Gone were all the challenges that my masochistic tendencies craved with a perhaps unhealthy urgency.

There were certainly masochistic challenges and problem solving to be had in the dirt, of course, but it wasn't the same. It wasn't the type that I *wanted*.

I enjoyed learning to ride dirt well enough, but my mind was still stuck in another place, not present for the experience I had. I guess that's how I've always been. Always looking forward, and always striving for just a little more. It wasn't the healthiest feeling, but my hustle mentality that had been ingrained in me since birth never went away, and anything that didn't further my ambitions felt like a sad waste of time sometimes. I needed more, and I had clear goals, and the pandemic had ripped those goals away in a way that no amount of fight and will power and distractions were allowed to take back.

As much as I had pushed this to the back of my mind all summer, it was at this end of the journey that I no longer had a place to hide. I couldn't just close my eyes and forget about it anymore.

Hollywood's birthday was coming up, too, and I knew that he would want to celebrate it somewhere at least a little special. And mine was just two months after his.

Birthdays were always kind of a weird thing for both of us. I know some people love their special day, and often celebrate their birth with a whole week or even a month of self-care, celebration, partying, and treating themselves. But for myself, since a young age, I'd always seen birthdays as a reminder of my own mortality. I never wanted to die, and to be reminded that I was always getting older was daunting and scary for the person who wanted to always hold onto their lust for life. Who never had enough time to do everything they wanted to do.

Which is why, in this pandemic, I couldn't justify locking myself in my house for the entire year as I was supposed to. To lose an ENTIRE year when I had such a finite number was the ultimate fear and torture for my mind, and I couldn't accept that as a reasonable suggestion. When everyone told me it was only two weeks, then only two months, then *only* six, as if that was no big deal, while they sat comfortably in the house they owned, working remotely at their secure job, and surrounded by their built family, it was a spit in the face for someone who was still actively building their own life, and needed every minute to get where they wanted to go.

One might say that it was a necessary inconvenience, and that anyone who couldn't handle indefinite lock down was selfish and evil, but I would sooner risk my body than my heart and mind. I'd risked my heart before, and that was far more likely to kill me than a bubonic plague itself.

So now, with little riding plans left, as I returned to Los Angeles, a city of endless quarantine and social policing from the most privileged among us, I felt trapped again.

"Why don't we go to Mexico for a little while?" I suggested, an absent gaze still fixated out the window. I'd been told the border was closed, but the real world experience of other riders painted a different picture. Surely we could cross. It's Mexico, after all. A country that actually had freedom, far unlike the one I lived in.

It didn't take much convincing to get Hollywood to agree.

Back in LA, we began preparing my 2015 Yamaha FZ-07 and Hollywood's 2003 Yamaha FZ1. We took our adventure gear out of storage, and we dusted off our road race helmets. We left our camping gear behind this time, figuring that hotels were inexpensive enough that we may as well just rely on those. It would be easier and require less preparation that way.

For the rest of my packing, ironically, I dusted off my first *Chronicles of a Motorcycle Gypsy* books to refresh my mind on my own pack list. The real value of recording a story is when you're scatter brained and bad at organization, but need to be ready to ride around the world in short order. Thanks slightly more focused past-Tiff!

Then in the last few days of October, we hopped back on our adventure steeds, and we headed south.

This whole summer had been to help my dirt riding on my big bike anyways. Where better to test out the transfer of my newfound skills than in Baja California?

The ride down was long and dull, and in about 30 seconds, we were officially over the border and riding through Tijuana. While I wasn't expecting rocket science, it was the easiest border crossing I've ever done in my life. We literally didn't even have to stop. No topes, no guards, no questions. The only challenge was dodging cars that paid no attention to the people on the tinier, more crushable vehicles. But otherwise, the border proved extremely not closed, to the point that they didn't even ask for a passport.

Having never been to this portion of the Pacific coast, we took the ocean road down, following a sweeping coastline amidst half built condos. A spectacle of endless blue oceans stretched out in my periphery, while the sound of crashing waves filled the air. This was more like the adventure I craved. Seeing new things in new places on new stretches of delicious asphalt. An hour through an unmanned toll road, and we arrived in the bustling cruise ship city of Ensenada.

I'd gotten an AirBNB that overlooked the ocean for Hollywood's birthday and we took a moment to readjust our standards and expectations to that of Mexico again. Last time we were in the Baja, we passed through Ensenada without so much as stopping, so it was interesting to spend a bit more time there. It still felt like a border town, with its dirt and grime and constant hustlers, looking to take money from the foreigners whenever they might let their guard down. We had to readjust to the broken and wildly uneven sidewalks, the layer of dirt on every surface, the sewer system that couldn't handle flushing toilet paper, non-potable water in the sink, and cohabitation with bugs. But food was unexpectedly top notch and the transition felt easy and natural.

We stopped in for a couple weeks, giving Hollywood time to fall in love with surfing, in between some day trips that reignited my love for my sporty, nimble parallel twin.

Hollywood celebrated his birthday riding the waves of Northern Mexico by day, and crashing a nearby birthday party for a cartel princess by night.

One idea was definitely better than the other, but even at the age of 38, I'm not sure Hollywood could distinguish which was which.

The weekend brought upon my first ever El Dia De Los Muertos south of the border, where I got the chance to forget for a few days that the whole world was shut down, while walking the pier among happy families and churros stuffed with cateja (a goat milk based caramel sauce). I even got sucked into a performance with a street clown, while Hollywood got his face painted so he could better startle unsuspecting children.

We hadn't intended to spend much more time in Ensenada, honestly, but about five days into our stay, that serendipity of travel life reared its beautiful head. Not even a mile from where we were staying, there was a motorcycle shop. That motorcycle shop just so happened to be owned by a Baja 1000 winner and current racer, and after my five year old stock battery on my FZ-07 unexpectedly died, he just so happened to be the nearest person who could get me one.

But want to know where it really got good? He was a good friend of one of our racing friends back in the states, and he was more than happy to let us tag along for the Baja 1000 race with his crew this year if we wanted to.

I'd never seen the Baja 1000 in person. Despite having lived so close to the Mexican border my whole life, it had never occurred to me that I could come down and hang out and watch the race. That was a bucket list item that might have been exciting enough to negate all of my bitching and whining about 2020. So to have the opportunity to get to watch the Baja 1000 for the first time from the perspective of the crew, who was working for one of the fastest motorcycle teams in the paddock no less?

My life is unreasonably wonderful sometimes.

We agreed eagerly, but with nearly a month until the race, we had a bit of time to kill. We didn't want to venture too far south, but being cramped in a hotel in Ensenada was quickly getting exhausting. We opted to make a quick ride down to San Quintin and back, and remember just a little bit what our travels used to feel like.

I'll just start by saying it felt so incredibly good. That freedom of the open road on a motorcycle is a sensation that's unmatched by anything other than wheels on pavement. Miles stretching behind me, exciting destinations inviting me up ahead. A world to discover on the back of my bike.

This kind of travel was my calling. It was everything I missed, and everything that had been taken away from me. Travelling in the states was fun, but there's a palpable difference between the world I grew up in versus a foreign place with foreign customs.

We followed a breathtaking coastline around wide open corners, then we took a dirt cut off to try out our skills off the beaten path. Rocks, sand, and massive rifts made up the road to the beach of La Lobera. I bounced along, allowing my wheels to move as needed, only struggling when my limited ground clearance pinged my underbody exhaust pipe.

I wasn't perfect off road on the FZ, and there came moments where the four wheel drive requirements far exceeded what was reasonable on my loaded naked sport bike, but gone was the intense fear that I once had when even traversing roads more simple than this. My skill and fear threshold was so dramatically improved, I was nearly thankful for having to delay my plans. Surely Siberia would be much more enjoyable with my new found confidence and ability.

My tires bounced and slid all the way back to the smooth paved highway, and I somehow didn't die.

I'm now almost as capable as my bike!

Once we had gotten our fill, hanging out in abandoned beach resorts and testing new skills, we returned to Ensenada, where I finished editing my third book about my travels in Asia, a story I called *Chronicles of a Mermaid*, then met up with Francisco Septian for our final briefing. The Baja 1000 had finally come. And I was ready to go.

While we didn't stay long, Swing Arm City was such a visual feast of an OHV park that I couldn't help wanting to stop, even if our bikes were extremely NOT suited to big hill climbs. (Swing Arm City, Utah)

Back on my sport bike and it feels so good! The Baja is always such a treat no matter what you're riding! (Ensenada, Mexico)

I think this is how I want to spend all of my winters from here on out. (San Quintin, Mexico)

The beaches of Baja never disappoint, and being able to handle some of the sand and stream crossings to get there without struggling has only made them sweeter. (El Rosario, Mexico)

I made it further down this rocky road on my FZ-07 than I ever could have hoped to do before—at least not without crying in my helmet. I was even riding hard enough to bottom my exhaust a few times, without being deterred! I think this dirt bike boot camp paid off! (La Lobera, Mexico)

When it started to get really rough, Hollywood offered to scout ahead. He came back a few minutes later shaking his head. So uh… this is where we turned around. (La Lobera, Mexico)

Back on the road, riding through foreign countries, adapting to changing conditions—this is my true happy place. I can only hope I'll soon be able to do this again in some new places. (San Quintin, Mexico)

Chapter 21

It was Thursday afternoon on the eve of the Baja 1000. The streets of Ensenada, Mexico were silent, save the usual hustle and bustle of daily life. There were no big crowds or vendors packing the streets with churros and colorful trinkets. It was a ghost town.

But while there may have been no fanfare or hype or glory in this uncertain world of November 2020, there was one thing you could always rely on—Racers were going to race.

It was 3:00AM when the chase van arrived outside our hotel in downtown Ensenada.

Team Elevators Etc included a three rider operation of Francisco Septian, Shane Esposito, and Justin Shultz, with two chase vehicles filled with friends, mechanics, and well… us. Ordinarily, the Baja 1000 had riders leaving Ensenada and barreling down the entirety of the peninsula until they arrived in the city of La Paz, approximately 1000 miles later (the route changes every year). But this year, because of COVID restrictions, they decided to just do an 898.40 mile loop through the mountains, on a course that was considered the most technically challenging to date. There were 187 total entries this year (versus last year's 273), from 14 countries and 26 states. A respectable showing, all things considered.

We climbed onto a bench seat with a group of upbeat mechanics who worked at Francisco's shop, Moto Garage 730.

"Are you ready for 24 hours of craziness?" The head mechanic asked, grinning back at us with a thumbs up.

I *thought* we were. But then, can you ever really be prepared for the chaos that is the Baja 1000?

At the Start/Finish line, the team chatted with Shane, the first rider up to bat, one last time before he left for the starting queue. Motorcycles and Quads would begin the race at 4:00AM, released in one-minute intervals. Trophy Trucks and UTVs wouldn't grid up until 10:00AM, so the riders would have enough of a head-start to gain a margin of safety. Having a 1200 horsepower trophy truck pass you on a narrow road, kicking up rocks the size of your head, isn't an ideal situation for... anyone, really. But definitely not for someone riding a cage-less, two wheeled vehicle.

Ordinarily, the start would be swamped with fans, but spectators were banned from the grid this year, including the rider's own team, so each rider launched into the dark unknown, HID headlights blaring, to the quiet applause of a handful of officials.

And then they were off. And we were off.

The crew ran to the van, everyone loading up as quickly as possible to begin the sprint to the first pit stop. We peeled out of the parking lot, rolled through Ensenada, and hopped onto Baja's Highway 1. Being in a chase vehicle is a race in and of itself, since if you don't get to each pit stop before your rider does, your rider will lose invaluable time that could cost them the entire race.

Our first stop took us to a restaurant about an hour out of town. The mountains were dark silhouettes in the distance, until the headlight of rider 1x lit up the mountainside. He descended the hills, then roared up a steep jump into the pit area. His bike bucked and slid its way onto the highway, as quickly as it had come. A few moments later, to the melody of crowing roosters under the pre-sunrise glow, our rider on 370x emerged from the trail.

In a split second, Shane dismounted the team's Honda CRF450X, Francisco hopped on, and the crew swapped out the headlight for a daytime configuration. With one last spin of a T-handle, Francisco took off on a six hour marathon.

Francisco had done many a Baja race before, which is why he had the foresight to establish the exact location of each pit stop in advanced. As a result, everyone knew exactly where to go, what part of the dirt they'd set up in, and what they would be doing when they got there. They were in it to win it, and if the rider had to slow down to look for their crew amongst a sea of competitor pits, they'd lose invaluable time.

The van weaved through lackadaisical Baja traffic, taking the bonus lane (By which I mean to say the shoulder. Or the dirt. Or the ditch and the weeds. Whatever didn't have blocking vehicles in it) past trains of semis, and occasionally cutting red lights by skirting the road entirely in the dirt. The world around the race operated as though nothing was happening at all, while the teams were on the ride of their life.

We watched as Francisco slid both tires through a turn, threading a needle into a tunnel beneath the highway, as his route crossed ours. On the next stop, his teammate tossed him a pair of daytime goggles, amidst the glaring reflection of the desert sand. We followed the Pacific Coast to San Quintin, then the course hooked back north to begin the loop.

Six hours and 300 miles down, we crunched through large, loose rocks to set up pit in a quarry. Here they would perform a rider and tire change. We all stepped back to avoid flying rocks as Francisco rode the bike onto the mat, then within a minute, they had a new rear wheel mounted and the chain lubed. Shane took over, riding into what was supposed to be one of the most challenging sections of the course. He bounced over whoops of rocks, wild yet in control, and we were back on the move.

While the next 100 miles was expected to take as long as 4 hours, which sounds like plenty of time, the next pit stop required a long haul over a twisting mountain pass of washboards and sand.

It was noon now, and every beater car in the Baja seemed to be out running errands. The lines of trucks were endless, as our driver carved around the caravans, screeching tires through the turns. We followed a pair of locals on dirt bikes down an unmarked road that would take us to the other side of the peninsula.

For hours, we twisted through those desert hills, passing Picacho Del Diablo, the highest peak in the Baja. Each jolt to the suspension reverberated through my spine, but we couldn't slow down. As we passed a small town, families stood outside their gates jumping up and down, smiling and waving at every chase vehicle that drove by. The crew waved back.

The Baja racers really were heroes out here.

But as endearing as that may be, there wasn't time to take it in. We barely arrived in time to meet our rider, as he came barreling into the pit before they even had time to set one up. Not the least of which because his front brakes had gone out.

They worked quickly to swap out the air filter, while Shane demonstrated the brake lever going straight to the handlebar. But with no way to fix it, he took off down the highway with only a rear brake to rely on. We followed behind him with our emergency flashers on, rolling at 60 kph (37 mph), which was the mandated speed whenever the riders were on the paved public motorways. (Each rider is equipped with a tracking device to assure they follow this rule).

Ten miles down the road, Francisco waved us off into the dirt. As luck would have it, a fellow racer with a spare Honda CRF450X agreed to help out. Within ten minutes (I timed it!), the master cylinder and brake lines were stripped from the parts bike, installed on the race bike, and fully bled and ready to go. Shane got back on the bike and tore into the course trying to make up time.

I've always loved this about the race community. Call it ego or call it sportsmanship, but no one wants to win a race because the other guy had a mechanical and couldn't make the grid, so racer's always help each other out. I don't know how many times I've had my own rivals help me up after a crash and hand me spare parts with a smile, and it was so great to see that this was the case even on this level. The racing community will always have my heart.

The Sea of Cortez was the next stop. The chase truck took off to the southern end of the San Felipe loop, and our van took off to the north exit, where we would be ready for another tire change. There wouldn't be enough time to get from one pit to the next if we stuck together, so this is where having two chase vehicles came in handy.

The sun set behind us as we parked at mile 660, sitting at the bottom of a sandy jump that was sure to be a spectacle. Hundreds of people were set up on either side of the course, campfires burning, mariachi music blasting, and laughter filling the air. You wouldn't even know the whole world had ended just a few months ago.

One hour passed. Then two. Then three. Still no sign of our rider. The "Weatherman" played over the radio, a channel where the crew could call in and ask for updates on their riders. "370X-ray is stopped at mile marker 567."

"That's us!" We pulled up live tracking through the SCORE app, and our rider was, indeed, stopped. Neither crew on either side knew why. We continued to watch, only to see he was now veering off course. Was he lost? Did he take a wrong turn?

Another tough part of the Baja is, when you're the crew and your rider is out on the course, there's nothing you can do to help them. We had no way to communicate or ask what was going on. A rider getting stranded out in the middle of the desert is a real risk, so much so, that it's required that you bring enough food and water to sustain you for a couple days if need be.

So we sat helplessly and waited.

With nothing we could do and exhaustion starting to set in, I took a power nap while another hour passed. At that point, our rider was back on track, blazing through the night at nearly 50 mph. When he arrived at our pit for a tire and rider change, we regrouped with the other chase truck to get the scoop. The brakes had failed again.

Fortunately, they had secured another parts bike, so this time they swapped the entire braking system from the caliper to the master cylinder, just in case the caliper had been the point of failure.

With new tires and a brake system secure, Francisco took over for the next section.

Justin, the last rider, debriefed as we packed up. He had run across a truck parked on the race course and accidentally ended up making a wrong turn as a result. The bike didn't have a GPS, so he was following signs that were left over from a Baja 500 race. He didn't realize he was lost until the tire tracks faded into cow tracks. The Baja is notorious for locals sabotaging the course to create a more exciting spectacle, sometimes digging holes or putting rocks on the route, and this may have been a case of exactly that.

It was midnight by the time we arrived at the next planned pit stop. Twenty hours since the start of the race and 200 miles still left to go. We waited by the fuel stop when Francisco came skidding in. Nothing wrong with the bike this time. The brakes had worked, the bike was fueled by a local operation who set up strategic fuel stops throughout the course, and just one last stretch was ahead. Shane took over for the last leg and took off chasing lost time. There was just one person he needed to pass to take the victory in their class.

Shane was a rider for Kawasaki and even raced the Dakar in the past. He was fast, and he was competitive. We raced ahead another hour down the road, just to make sure he was in good shape, but as he blasted by us, within feet of the pit, we knew he had it handled.

I fell asleep on the 2 hour drive back to Ensenada. The whole crew did. Then we pulled into Moto Garage 730 at 5:30AM. Shane rolled in shortly after, with the elation of someone who had just finished 898.40 miles of one of the most intense, dangerous, and grueling races in the world.

The total time? 24:32.19.

At the end of the day, it's not where you finish in the Baja that matters. It's that you finished at all. Sure it's impressive to come in first, and everyone wants a coveted spot on the podium, but to simply stand on your own two feet after all those hours of rocks and sand and mishaps, alive and successful, is the greatest victory of all.

Although our team did, in fact, take first in their class, so winning is pretty great, too!

I came to the Baja a month prior with the intention of simply settling down, getting just a sampling of the motorcycle travel life I so missed. But instead, I found myself in a crazy whirlwind of fast bikes, faster riders, and the cheering of Mexican Spectators. While I'm sure it was nothing compared to the fanfare of pre-pandemic times, for the racers themselves, it's still every bit as grueling, intense, and satisfying.

It was amazing to get check "Watch a Baja 1000 race" off my bucket list in the coolest way possible! Now I might just have to add racing in it!

I've seen some parties in Mexico, and they definitely never looked like this. But the parties in the desert still raged hard. The people of Mexico definitely love their desert racing. (Ensenada, Mexico)

The calm before the storm at the starting line was especially calm this year, with no spectators allowed. But racers will race even if no one ever watches. (Ensenada, Mexico)

For fuel, some riders have their pit crew haul around 5 gallon jugs, but there's also a company who sets up quick fueling pits every 50 miles or so that takes the headache out of it. (Baja, Mexico)

The course covered everything from hard pack to soft sand to deep ruts to rocks, and the riders had to be fast and confident in all of it. It's difficult to watch most of the race, since it covers so much ground. But that brief moment when a racer buzzes you is exhilarating. (Baja, Mexico)

For the racers among us who are ballin' on a very large budget, you can also hire a helicopter as your chase vehicle. (Baja, Mexico)

Set up and ready for the first tire and air filter change! (Baja, Mexico)

The crew functioned like a well-oiled machine, through hold ups and mechanicals and everything in between. (Baja, Mexico)

You're only allowed one bike for the race (They mark the engines to assure you don't change them), but many teams travelled with spare bikes so they wouldn't have to worry about missing the needed parts. Fortunately, those racers also don't mind sharing when they come across another racer in need. (Baja, Mexico)

The last tire change of the race (They swapped every ~300 miles) was under head lamps somewhere around midnight. (Baja, Mexico)

Huge thanks and congratulations to the whole team at Elevators Etc and Moto Garage 730! (Ensenada, Mexico)

Chapter 22

After the Baja 1000 concluded, still riding high, we headed back to the states to spend the holidays with family. Still being so close to home, it was somehow a much more appealing idea to eat a full American Thanksgiving meal of turkey and stuffing and mashed potatoes and pumpkin pie than it was to pass the day with tacos and flan. We'd get plenty of those in the coming months.

We stayed through Christmas, taking a few days here and there along the way to ride in the desert with friends in the now mild temperatures of Southern California in December. Chris and Sara, the French couple who we had met in Johnson Valley, met us at Rowher Flats for a long ride up into the trees. Another day, I got the privilege to bring my mom into the hills, and teach her to ride a dirt bike for the first time.

I'd shared a lot with my mother in my life, and she was truly one of my best friends. So to get to introduce her to motorcycles, the passion that has shaped my entire lifestyle, was among the happiest moments of the entire year for me. She took to the little KLX125 perhaps more easily than I did, and she even did an accidental wheelie!

In all the devastation of 2020, this was like a gold star, shining brightly in the darkness.

Another day, my old friend Slim, a road racer who I had known for a solid decade now, met us at Lake Arrowhead for a quick jaunt through the hills. Though after a day of waiting for me to pick my lines around the dips and ruts, he insisted on letting me borrow one of his spare dirt bikes. The next time we rode together, he showed up with a bright red Honda CRF230F, and he wouldn't let me leave the lot without it.

After the hubbub of Christmas, it was my birthday, December 29th, when I finally graduated.

In the deep deserts of Ridgecrest California, a hundred miles from anything, we parked our truck in the sand. To each side of me were trucks, vans, and campers of long time friends from the racetrack, who had all switched to riding dirt in recent years. Some simply because it was cheaper than the road racing world, others for a new challenge. Stacy made hot chocolate, while Hollywood built a fire in the frigid December night in the high Californian desert. Temperatures knocked on freezing, while the laughs of friends I hadn't seen since I left on my first motorcycle journey, all those years ago, warmed my heart from the inside out.

As I turned 33 years old, I threw my leg over the tall seat of that red Honda. I stood tall on the pegs of a bike that was physically sized just right for my adult frame. I felt my large diameter tires roll over every imperfection in the desert with ease. I'd come full circle from my first dirt experience, and I was finally ready for it.

In a sense, it felt a little bit like learning to ride dirt all over again, having none of the long learned confidence I had developed on my bike that was tiny, reassuring, and familiar. But in every other sense, it felt like a step torward becoming a better and more well-rounded rider, who could truly take on any task or obstacle that came my way.

This year of uncertainty, pandemics, and lock downs had taken a huge toll on everything I held dear. From my life goals, to my mental health, to my relationships, nothing was certain, nothing worked out quite as I had hoped, and every happy moment was tainted with stress and confusion.

But today, I wasn't confused. I was strong and I was confident and I was capable. I'd forever have a long way to go in learning to ride dirt bikes and motorcycles. I had an even longer way to go in learning to balance my happiness, security, and travel, particularly after having now lived the experience of giving up my home and comfort and our livelihood at the worst possible moment, where I found myself unable to lean on anyone but the closest family. The highs and lows were a constant whirlwind that never slowed or lightened in force.

But maybe all of that is just part of the journey. Whether I'm lost in Siberia or lost in my own head, maybe having to overcome the extreme pain and hardships of failure and disappointment are what the travel life has always been about, no matter where I am and what I'm doing.

Whatever the case, I decided to keep looking up, do my best to ignore the doomsday politics, and keep hoping that the border issues improve. There's still a big world out there to see, and now I'm way more prepared to see it!

There's no better way to start a new year of life and a new year, period, than with new and old friends alike—particularly if they're all riding motorcycles. (Ridgecrest, California)

After a decade or so of track days and racing, I was starting to find that a lot of my friends had gotten dirt bikes to explore something new. Sharing the sport with likeminded people has always been a huge draw of riding for me, and now I could finally enjoy dirt with my racetrack friends! (Lake Arrowhead, California)

Teaching my mom to ride, sharing the thing I'm most passionate about with the person who means the most to me, might have been the greatest blessing in all the curses that were the year 2020. (Rowher Flats, California)

My journey to learn to ride a dirt bike was rarely easy, but it's a skill that I know will serve me well in my future travels, both foreign and domestic. I don't know what my future travels will bring, or if they'll ever be like they were before the pandemic rattled my entire life, but I do know that I'm proud of what I accomplished, even if this is only the beginning of this new facet of my riding career. (Ridgecrest, California)

Epilogue

After the first of the year passed, with months ticking by with no end to the pandemic in sight, my mental health dropped back to a low that was all too frequent lately, and it was about time we made a decision about what came next. With borders still closed, an impenetrable housing and rental market, and a dead job market, there was only one place we *could* go:

South.

There was a lot I hadn't seen in Mexico my first time through. There were tons of places I hadn't explored, history I hadn't learned, and roads that I had been too intimidated to give a second glance. And with one single state in Mexico I had never been to, it only seemed right to finish the job.

With uncertainty in our minds and hope in our hearts, we twisted our throttles into the horizon. For the first time in a long time, I was truly excited about the possibilities again. If nothing else, I was ready to escape our country for a little while, and the divided mess that it had become. Because south, there were still possibilities. Maybe I would ride to Cancun. Maybe it would be Panama. Hell, if South America ever opens its borders again, maybe it'll be Tierra Del Fuego! Whatever the case, I was open to giving myself to this uncertain future, whatever it might hold.

Trails!

So, since the pack list for this installment isn't particularly interesting or useful, I thought it might be more helpful to include the trail names for all of the places I rode this year! In the order that I rode them, here's everywhere, from beginning to end of this dirt bike boot camp!

1) Wolford Reservoir: Kremmling, Colorado
2) North Fork of Tiger Road: Breckenridge, Colorado
3) Snyder's Creek: Gould, Colorado
4) Tiger Road, Various: Breckenridge, Colorado
5) North Sand Hills Recreation Management Area: Walden, Colorado
6) Shoshone National Forest: Dubois, Wyoming
7) Norwegian Gulch: Augusta, Montana
8) Fresno OHV: Havre, Montana
9) Glasgow OHV: Glasgow, Montana
10) Fresno Lake: Havre, Montana
11) Stanley Lake: Stanley Lake, Idaho
12) Baumgartner: Featherville, Idaho
13) Elk City: Elk City, Idaho
14) Silverton: Telluride, Colorado
15) Ouray: Ouray, Colorado
16) Crested Butte: Crested Butte, Colorado
17) Gold Mountain: Big Bear, California
18) Cougar Butte: Johnson Valley, California
19) Hurrah Pass: Moab, Utah
20) Kokopelli Trail: Moab, Utah
21) Seven Mile Rim: Moab Utah
22) Slick Rock: Moab, Utah
23) Swing Arm City: Hanksville, Utah
24) La Lobera, Baja California
25) Lake Arrowhead: Lake Arrowhead, California
26) Rowher Flats: Santa Clarita, California
27) Ridgecrest: Ridgecrest, California

Final Thoughts

Another year, another book! I'm sure we're all still reeling from 2020, even as we approach 2022, and I know that even now, I still don't know what I'm doing and where I'm going. A lot changed for me this last year and a half. I've continued writing, having now completed something like 13 books, both fiction and nonfiction. I had my first Romance Novel under a traditional publishing contract come out this last year. I've started a series about cats in the zombie apocalypse (as someone whose first professional nickname was Zombie because of my love of Resident Evil, that's a bit of a passion project), and have been writing as much as I can squeeze in between my otherwise tumultuous life.

I also started writing for Revzilla's Common Tread on a somewhat regular basis! They've been so much fun to work with, and it's been great to continue to share some essays and opinions and stories on a larger platform. Between journalism and authorship, I'm slowly but surely learning to navigate this messy world of calling myself a writer.

On the motorcycle front, I just finished 6 months of riding in Mexico, and am currently sorting out the next step as borders continue to be closed. That savings is just about depleted and some big questions will have to be answered soon, but as we always do, we pick ourselves up and start over. Hollywood accepted a job in Pueblo, Colorado, so I'll be trying to actually live in Colorado full time for the first time ever, and I'm hoping it's as wonderful as my past visits have been. I'm looking forward to sampling both more of the riding there and perhaps venturing into New Mexico more in the coming months. Things always work out, it seems. That kind of serendipity of life is always what keeps me going, no matter how dark it gets.

All I can hope now is that, one day, we'll be back to being able to travel freely so I can finally jump to a new continent. I'm still dying to see Russia, and the Russian Embassy is still waiting to issue my visa.

All that said, if you enjoyed this book, please leave a review! It's a huge help, and I always like getting feedback so I can improve on my craft. Otherwise, if you want to follow my future adventures or chat about scuba diving or motorcycles or whatever, you can follow and/or message me on social media through all the usual channels! I'm always excited to hear from people, even if sometimes it takes me a minute to get the time and WiFi!

Instagram: https://www.instagram.com/tiffaniburkett/

Facebook: https://www.facebook.com/tiffaniburkettFZ07/

Twitter: https://twitter.com/BurkettTiffani

Youtube: https://www.youtube.com/channel/UC0Cv9VxKEyrYu6dfa0Awj5w

Thanks so much for reading! Until next time, go fast and take chances!

Made in United States
North Haven, CT
05 December 2021

12046069R00176